Landauer Books

THIMBLEBERRIES

Making *your* House

A Home

This book was produced, and published by Landauer Books
A division of Landauer Corporation
3100 101st Street, Urbandale, IA 50322
www.landauercorp.com   800/557-2144

President/Publisher: Jeramy Lanigan Landauer
Director of Sales and Operations: Kitty Jacobson
Managing Editor: Jeri Simon
Art Director: Laurel Albright

For Thimbleberries®:
Creative Director: Lynette Jensen
Photographer: Keith Evenson
Photostyling: Lynette Jensen
Technical Writer: Sue Bahr
Technical Illustrator: Lisa Kirchoff

ISBN 13: 978-0-9800688-2-5
ISBN 10:   0-9800688-2-7

Library of Congress Control Number: 2008926902

This book printed on acid-free paper.
Printed in China

10-9-8-7-6-5-4-3-2-1

THIMBLEBERRIES®

Making *your* House

A Home

by Lynette Jensen

a home decorating notebook

Cool Breeze

100 x 108-inches

. . . warm up with Cool Breeze on a summer night.

Cool Breeze

100 x 108-inches

Fabrics and Supplies

4-1/4 yards **BLUE/CREAM FLORAL** for quilt center and outer border
(cut on the lengthwise grain)

7/8 yard **BLUE/GREEN LEAF PRINT** for quilt center

1 yard **SMALL BLUE/PLUM FLORAL** for quilt center and corner squares

2-1/3 yards **LARGE BLUE FLORAL** for vertical lattice strips
(cut on the lengthwise grain)

1-1/8 yards **GREEN PRINT** for inner border

3/4 yard **BLUE DOT** for middle border

1 yard **GREEN PRINT** for binding

9 yards **BLUE/GREEN LEAF PRINT** for backing
OR
3-1/4 yards of 108-inch wide fabric for backing

quilt batting, at least 106 x 114 -inches

Before beginning this project, read through General Instructions on page 62.

Quilt Center

The yardage given allows for the **BLUE/CREAM FLORAL** <u>wide outer border strips</u> *and the* **LARGE BLUE FLORAL** <u>vertical lattice strips</u> *to be cut on the lengthwise grain (a couple extra inches are allowed for trimming). Cutting these strips lengthwise will eliminate the need for piecing. The remaining pieces for the quilt center should be cut on the crosswise grain.*

Cutting

From **BLUE/CREAM FLORAL**:
- Cut a 3-1/8 yard piece (44 x 112-inches) and set aside to be used for the outer border which will be cut on the lengthwise grain.
- From the remaining 1-1/8 yard piece, cut 4, 8-1/2 x 44-inch strips. From the strips cut: 16, 8-1/2-inch squares

From **BLUE/GREEN LEAF PRINT**:
- Cut 3, 8-1/2 x 44-inch strips. From the strips cut: 12, 8-1/2-inch squares

From **SMALL BLUE/PLUM FLORAL**:
- Cut 3, 8-1/2 x 44-inch strips. From the strips cut: 12, 8-1/2-inch squares

From **LARGE BLUE FLORAL**:
- Cut 5, 8-1/2 x 83-inch vertical lattice strips (cut on the lengthwise grain)

Piecing

Step 1 Referring to the quilt center assembly diagram for block placement, sew the 8-1/2-inch squares together in 4 vertical block rows; press. <u>At this point each vertical block row should measure 8-1/2 x 80-1/2-inches.</u>

Step 2 Cut the 8-1/2 x 83-inch **LARGE BLUE FLORAL** vertical lattice strips to the length of your block rows. Lay out the **LARGE BLUE FLORAL** vertical lattice strips and the vertical block rows. *Note: The* **LARGE BLUE FLORAL** *strips may appear directional so pay attention to this detail.* Sew the lattice strips and the block rows together to make the quilt center; press. <u>At this point the quilt center should measure 72-1/2 x 80-1/2-inches.</u>

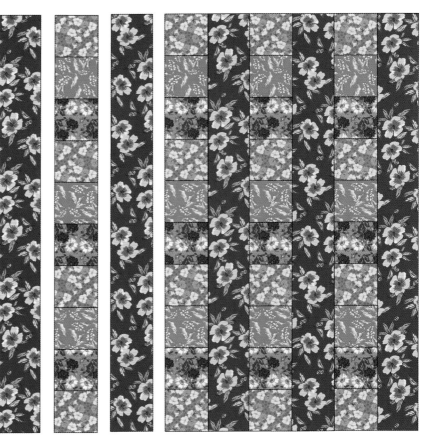

Quilt Center Assembly Diagram

Borders

Note: The yardage given allows for the **BLUE/CREAM FLORAL** <u>wide outer border strips</u> *to be cut on the lengthwise grain (a couple extra inches are allowed for trimming). Cutting the wide border strips lengthwise will eliminate the need for piecing. The yardage given allows for the* <u>narrow inner and middle border strips</u> *to be cut on the crosswise grain. Diagonally piece the strips as needed, referring to* **Diagonal Piecing** *instructions on page 75. Read through* **Border** *instructions on page 73 for general instructions on adding borders.*

Cutting

From **GREEN PRINT**:
- Cut 8, 4-1/2 x 44-inch inner border strips

From **SMALL BLUE/PLUM FLORAL**:
- Cut 4, 4-1/2-inch corner squares

From **BLUE DOT**:
- Cut 9, 2-1/2 x 44-inch middle border strips

From **BLUE/CREAM FLORAL**:
- Cut 2, 8-1/2 x 112-inch side outer border strips
  (cut on the lengthwise grain)
- Cut 2, 8-1/2 x 87-inch top/bottom outer border strips
  (cut on the lengthwise grain)

Attaching the Borders

Step 1 Attach the 4-1/2-inch wide **GREEN** top/bottom inner border strips.

Step 2 For the side borders, measure the quilt from top to bottom through the middle including the seam allowances, but not the borders just added. Cut the 4-1/2-inch wide **GREEN** side border strips to this length. Sew a 4-1/2-inch **SMALL BLUE/PLUM FLORAL** corner square to both ends of the side border strips; press. Sew the borders to the side edges of the quilt; press.

Step 3 Attach the 2-1/2-inch wide **BLUE DOT** middle border strips.

Step 4 Attach the 8-1/2-inch wide **BLUE/CREAM FLORAL** outer border strips.

Putting It All Together

- If you are using 108-inch wide backing fabric, simply trim the backing and batting so they are 3-inches larger on all 4 sides than the quilt top.
- If you are using 44-inch wide backing fabric, cut the 9 yard length of backing fabric in thirds crosswise to make 3, 3 yard lengths.
- Refer to **Finishing the Quilt** on page 75 for complete instructions.

Finished Back Diagram

44″

3 yd

3 yd

3 yd

108″

132″

Quilt

seam

seam

44-inch wide fabric

108″

117″

Quilt

108-inch wide fabric

Quilting Suggestions:

- Quilt center vertical block rows - alternate horizontal channel stitches, vertical channel stitches, and a big X in the individual squares.
- **LARGE BLUE FLORAL** vertical lattice strips - meander.
- **GREEN** inner border - **TB48 Border Heart**.
- **SMALL BLUE/PLUM FLORAL** corner squares - big X.
- **BLUE DOT** middle border - **TB30 Beadwork**.
- **BLUE/CREAM FLORAL** outer border - meander.

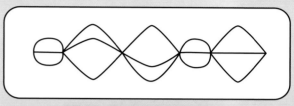

TB 30   Beadwork (1-1/2″)

TB 48   Border Hearts (3-1/2″)

THIMBLEBERRIES® quilt stencils by Quilting Creations International are available at your local quilt shop.

Binding

Cutting

From **GREEN PRINT**:
- Cut 10 to 11, 2-3/4 x 44-inch strips

Sew the binding to the quilt using a 3/8-inch seam allowance. This measurement will produce a 1/2-inch wide finished double binding. Refer to **Binding** and **Diagonal Piecing** on page 75 for complete instructions.

Cool Breeze
100 x 108-inches

A simple gathered dust ruffle made from a coordinating print always completes a bed ensemble.

Dust Ruffle

for queen bed with an 18-inch drop

Fabrics and Supplies

6-1/2 yards **CREAM PRINT** for dust ruffle

3-3/4 yards **BEIGE PRINT** for center panel

quilting thread or cording for gathering the dust ruffle

Before beginning this project, read through
General Instructions on page 62.

Photographed on page 8.

Special Measuring Instructions

*If your drop length differs from 18-inches, use the
following instructions to determine the correct drop
length of your dust ruffle.*

Step 1 Measure from the top edge of the box spring
to the floor; add 2-1/2-inches to allow for a hem and
seam allowance.

Step 2 For ease in construction, make the dust ruffle
in 3 sections - 2 for the sides and one for the foot end.
To determine the number of fabric strips to cut for the
dust ruffle, measure the side of your box spring and
multiply this length by 2 or 2-1/2, depending on the
fullness you want and the weight of your fabric. Repeat
for the other side and the foot end of the bed. Add these
measurements together to get the total inches needed.

Step 3 Cut and piece the strips of fabric according to
the measurements determined in Steps 1 and 2.

Center Panel

Step 1 Cut the 3-3/4 yard length of **BEIGE PRINT** in
half crosswise to make 2, 1-7/8 yard lengths. Sew the long
edges together; press. Trim the **BEIGE PRINT** to
61 x 80-3/4-inches.

*Note: If your mattress size differs from 60 x 78-inches,
measure the width and length of the bed's box spring.
Add 1-inch to the width measurement and 2-3/4-inches
to the length measurement to allow for a hem and seam
allowance. Cut a piece of **BEIGE PRINT** according to
this measurement to make the center panel.*

Step 2 Turn one short edge of the **BEIGE PRINT**
under 1/4-inch; press. Turn the same edge under another
2-inches; press. Stitch the folded edge in place to hem
the top edge of the center panel.

Step 3 Measure the side of the center panel, from point A
to point B. Divide the measurement by 4; mark those points

---

on the side raw edges of the center
panel. Repeat for the other side
(point C to point D) and the foot
end (point B to point C).

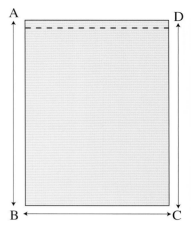

Make the Dust Ruffle

*Note: For ease in construction,
make the dust ruffle in 3 sections -
2 for the sides and one for the
foot end.*

Cutting

From **CREAM PRINT**:
- Cut 8, 20-1/2 x 44-inch strips. Piece 4 of the strips
  together for each side.
- Cut 3 more 20-1/2 x 44-inch strips. Piece the strips
  together for the foot end.

Piecing

Step 1 Working with one side section, turn a long edge of the
dust ruffle under 1-inch; press. Turn the same edge under
another 1-inch; press. Stitch the folded edge in place to hem
the lower edge. Make a 1-inch double hem for each short edge.
Divide the top edge of the dust ruffle
into fourths; mark with safety pins.
Press, sew, and mark the remaining
side section and foot end section in
the same manner.

raw edge

Double 1-inch hem at long edge
and 2 short ends

Step 2 To gather the dust ruffle, position 2 strands of quilting
thread (or cording) 1/4-inch from the raw edge. The length of
the thread for each side section should be 160-inches long and
120-inches long for the foot end section. Stitch across one end
of the thread to secure it in place. To gather the fabric, zigzag
stitch over the length of thread, pushing the fabric onto the
thread as you continue stitching. Refer to ruffle diagram on
page 39.

Step 3 With right sides together
and raw edges aligned, place a
dust ruffle section on the center
panel, matching marks and pin,
referring to the diagram. Pull the
thread to gather the dust ruffle
into an even fit; pin in place.
Sew the dust ruffle section to the
center panel with a 1/2-inch seam
allowance. Repeat to sew the
remaining sections to the center
panel to complete the dust ruffle.

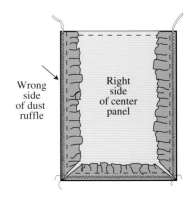

Wrong
side
of dust
ruffle

Right
side
of center
panel

Step 4 Position the dust ruffle on the box spring. Position the
mattress on top. Adjust the dust ruffle as needed.

Garden Secret Runner

30 x 40-inches

. . . a runner or a wall quilt.

Garden Secret Runner

30 x 40-inches

 abrics and Supplies

1/2 yard **BEIGE DOT** for center panel and hourglass blocks

3/8 yard **RED PRINT** for center panel and hourglass blocks

3/4 yard **RED/CREAM FLORAL** for hourglass blocks and outer border

1/4 yard **GOLD PRINT** for hourglass blocks

1/4 yard **SMALL RED/GREEN FLORAL** for hourglass blocks

1/4 yard **OLIVE GREEN FLORAL** for hourglass blocks

1/4 yard **GREEN STRIPE** for inner border

3/8 yard **RED PRINT** for binding

1 yard **SMALL RED/GREEN FLORAL** for backing

quilt batting, at least 36 x 46-inches

Before beginning this project, read through General Instructions on page 62.

Center Panel

Cutting

From BEIGE DOT:
- Cut 1, 8-1/2 x 18-1/2-inch center rectangle
- Cut 4, 4-1/2-inch squares

From RED PRINT:
- Cut 1, 4-1/2 x 44-inch strip. From the strip cut:
  2, 4-1/2 x 8-1/2-inch rectangles
  2, 2-1/2 x 8-1/2-inch rectangles

Piecing

Step 1 Position a 4-1/2-inch **BEIGE DOT** square on the corner of a 4-1/2 x 8-1/2 **RED PRINT** rectangle. Draw a diagonal line on the square and stitch on the line. Trim the seam allowance to 1/4-inch; press. Repeat this process at the opposite corner of the rectangle.

Make 2

Step 2 Sew the Step 1 units to both ends of the 8-1/2 x 18-1/2-inch **BEIGE DOT** rectangle; press.

Step 3 Sew the 2-1/2 x 8-1/2-inch **RED PRINT** rectangles to both ends of the center unit; press. At this point the center panel should measure 8-1/2 x 30-1/2-inches.

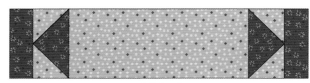

Make 1

Hourglass Blocks

Makes 10 blocks

Cutting

From BEIGE DOT:
- Cut 2, 7-1/4-inch squares. Cut the squares diagonally into quarters to make 8 triangles. You will be using only 6 triangles.

From RED PRINT:
- Cut 2, 7-1/4-inch squares. Cut the squares diagonally into quarters to make 8 triangles. You will be using only 6 triangles.

From RED/CREAM FLORAL:
- Cut 2, 7-1/4-inch squares. Cut the squares diagonally into quarters to make 8 triangles. You will be using only 6 triangles.

From GOLD PRINT:
- Cut 2, 7-1/4-inch squares. Cut the squares diagonally into quarters to make 8 triangles. You will be using only 6 triangles.

From SMALL RED/GREEN FLORAL:
- Cut 2, 7-1/4-inch squares. Cut the squares diagonally into quarters to make 8 triangles.

From OLIVE GREEN FLORAL:
- Cut 2, 7-1/4-inch squares. Cut the squares diagonally into quarters to make 8 triangles.

Piecing

Step 1 With right sides together, layer a **BEIGE DOT** triangle on a **RED PRINT** triangle. Stitch along the bias edge being careful not to stretch the triangles. Press the seam allowance toward the **RED** triangle. Repeat for the remaining **BEIGE DOT** and **RED** triangles. Make 6 triangle units. Sew the triangle units together in pairs; press. At this point each hourglass block should measure 6-1/2-inches square.

Bias edges

Make 6 triangle units   Make 3 hourglass blocks

Step 2 With right sides together, layer a **GOLD PRINT** triangle on a **RED/CREAM FLORAL** triangle. Stitch along the bias edge. Press the seam allowance toward the **RED/CREAM FLORAL** triangle. Repeat for the remaining **GOLD PRINT** and **RED/CREAM FLORAL** triangles. Make 6 triangle units. Sew the triangle units together in pairs; press. At this point each hourglass block should measure 6-1/2-inches square.

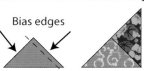

Bias edges

Make 6 triangle units   Make 3 hourglass blocks

Step 3 With right sides together, layer a **SMALL RED/ GREEN FLORAL** triangle on an **OLIVE**

GREEN FLORAL triangle. Stitch along the bias edge. Press the seam allowance toward the SMALL RED/GREEN FLORAL triangle. Repeat for the remaining SMALL RED/GREEN FLORAL and OLIVE GREEN FLORAL triangles. Make 8 triangle units. Sew the triangle units together in pairs; press. At this point each hourglass block should measure 6-1/2-inches square.

Make 8
triangle units

Make 4
hourglass blocks

Step 4 Referring to the runner diagram for block placement, sew together 5 of the hourglass blocks for each side of the runner center; press. At this point each hourglass strip should measure 6-1/2 x 30-1/2-inches. Sew the hourglass strips to both side edges of the runner center; press. At this point the runner center should measure 20-1/2 x 30-1/2-inches.

Make 1

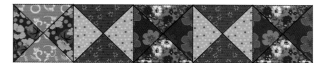

Make 1

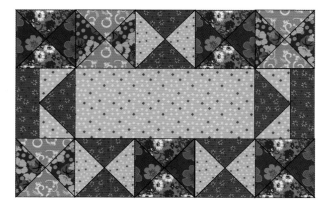

Runner Center

Borders

Note: *Read through* **Border** *instructions on page 73 for general instructions on adding borders.*

Cutting
From **GREEN STRIPE**:
• Cut 3, 1-1/2 x 44-inch inner border strips

From **RED/CREAM FLORAL**:
• Cut 4, 4-1/2 x 44-inch outer border strips

Attaching the Borders
Step 1 Attach the 1-1/2-inch wide **GREEN STRIPE** inner border strips.

Step 2 Attach the 4-1/2-inch wide **RED/CREAM FLORAL** outer border strips.

Quilting Suggestions:
• **BEIGE DOT** center rectangle - **TB25 Connecting Maze**
• **RED** flying geese - echo quilt
• **BEIGE DOT** flying geese background— echo quilt
• **RED** rectangles - 7/8-inch wide channel stitch
• Hourglass blocks - **TB 4 Wings** and **TB 17 Lady Slipper**
• **GREEN STRIPE** inner border - in-the-ditch on both sides
• **RED/CREAM FLORAL** outer border - **TB48 Border Heart**

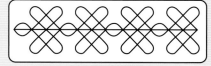

TB 25 Connecting Maze (5")

TB 48 Border Hearts (3-1/2")

TB 4 Wings (5")

TB 17 Lady Slipper (5")

THIMBLEBERRIES® quilt stencils by Quilting Creations International are available at your local quilt shop.

Putting It All Together

Trim the batting and backing so they are 4-inches larger than the runner top. Refer to **Finishing the Quilt** on page 75 for complete instructions.

Binding

Cutting

From **RED PRINT**:

• Cut 4, 2-3/4 x 44-inch strips

Sew the binding to the quilt using a 3/8-inch seam allowance. This measurement will produce a 1/2-inch wide finished double binding. Refer to **Binding** and **Diagonal Piecing** on page 75 for instructions.

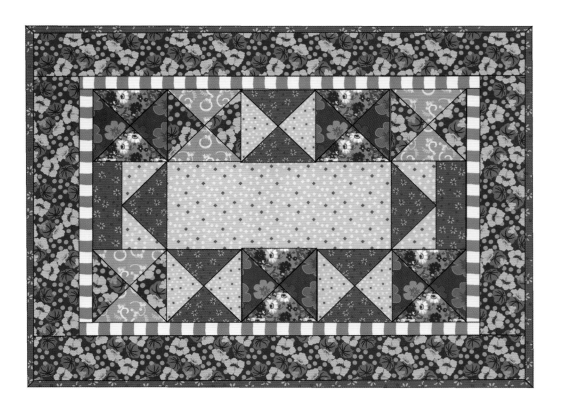

Garden Secret Runner
30 x 40-inches

14

Garden Secret Runner

2nd Color Option

30 x 40-inches

Fabrics and Supplies

1/2 yard **LIGHT GOLD PRINT** for center panel and hourglass blocks

3/8 yard **GREEN PRINT** for center panel and hourglass blocks

3/4 yard **RUST PRINT** for hourglass blocks and outer border

1/4 yard **DARK GOLD PRINT** for hourglass blocks

1/4 yard **ORANGE PRINT** for hourglass blocks

1/4 yard **RED PRINT** for hourglass blocks

1/4 yard **BLACK PRINT** for inner border

3/8 yard **GREEN PRINT** for binding

1 yard **ORANGE PRINT** for backing

quilt batting, at least 36 x 46-inches

Before beginning this project, read through General Instructions on page 62.

Sunsplashed

90 x 110-inches

. . . total ease and comfort.

Sunsplashed

90 x 110-inches

abrics and Supplies

4-1/8 yards **LARGE RED FLORAL** for pieced blocks and outer border
(cut on the lengthwise grain)

2/3 yard **RED PRINT** for pieced blocks

1 yard **OLIVE GREEN FLORAL** for pieced blocks and narrow middle border

2-1/8 yards **RED/CREAM FLORAL** for pieced blocks and wide middle border

1/2 yard **GOLD PRINT** for pieced blocks and corner squares

1/2 yard **BEIGE/GREEN LEAF PRINT** for pieced blocks

3/4 yard **BEIGE DOT** for pieced blocks and inner border

1/2 yard **SMALL RED/GREEN FLORAL** for pieced blocks

1 yard **OLIVE GREEN FLORAL** for binding

8 yards **RED/CREAM FLORAL** for backing

OR

3-1/4 yards of 108-inch wide fabric for backing

quilt batting, at least 96 x 116 -inches

Before beginning this project, read through General Instructions on page 62.

Quilt Center

*The yardage given allows for the **LARGE RED FLORAL** <u>wide outer border strips</u> to be cut on the lengthwise grain (a couple extra inches are allowed for trimming). Cutting these strips lengthwise will eliminate the need for piecing. The remaining pieces for the quilt should be cut on the crosswise grain.*

Cutting

From **LARGE RED FLORAL**:
- Cut a 3-1/8 yard piece (44 x 112-inches) and set aside to be used for the outer border, which will be cut on the lengthwise grain.
- From the remaining 1 yard piece, cut 3, 10-1/2 x 44-inch strips (cut on the crosswise grain). From these strips cut:
     10, 8-1/2 x 10-1/2-inch rectangles

From **RED PRINT**:
- Cut 2, 4-1/2 x 44-inch strips
- Cut 4, 2-1/2 x 44-inch strips.
     From the strips cut:
     13, 2-1/2 x 10-1/2-inch rectangles
     8, 2-1/2-inch squares

From **OLIVE GREEN FLORAL**:
- Cut 4, 2-1/2 x 44-inch strips.
     From the strips cut:
     16, 2-1/2 x 8-1/2-inch rectangles

From **RED/CREAM FLORAL**:
- Cut 1, 8-1/2 x 44-inch strip.
     From the strip cut:
     3, 8-1/2 x 10-1/2-inch rectangles
- Cut 2 more 8-1/2 x 44-inch strips.
     From the strips cut:
     8, 8-1/2-inch squares

From **GOLD PRINT**:
- Cut 1, 6-1/2 x 44-inch strip

From **BEIGE/GREEN LEAF PRINT**:
- Cut 2, 6-1/2 x 44-inch strips.
     From the strips cut:
     8, 6-1/2 x 10-1/2-inch rectangles

From **BEIGE DOT**:
- Cut 1, 6-1/2 x 44-inch strip

From **SMALL RED/GREEN FLORAL**:
- Cut 2, 6-1/2 x 44-inch strips.
     From the strips cut:
     8, 6-1/2 x 10-1/2-inch rectangles

Piecing - Block A, makes 10 blocks

Sew 10 of the 2-1/2 x 10-1/2-inch **RED PRINT** rectangles to the top edge of the 8-1/2 x 10-1/2-inch **LARGE RED FLORAL** rectangles; press. <u>At this point each Block A should measure 10-1/2-inches square.</u>

Block A, make 10

Piecing - Block B, makes 8 blocks

Step 1 Sew 8 of the 2-1/2 x 8-1/2-inch **OLIVE GREEN** rectangles to the top edge of 8 of the 8-1/2-inch **RED/CREAM FLORAL** squares. Press the seam allowances toward the **OLIVE GREEN** rectangles.

Make 8

Step 2 Sew 2-1/2-inch **RED PRINT** squares to the left edge of 8 of the 2-1/2 x 8-1/2-inch **OLIVE GREEN** rectangles. Press the seam allowances toward the **OLIVE GREEN** rectangles. Sew these units to the left edge of the Step 1 units; press. <u>At this point each Block B should measure 10-1/2-inches square.</u>

Make 8

Block B, make 8

Step 3 Referring to the diagram for block placement, sew together 6 of the A Blocks and the 8 B Blocks in 2 vertical block rows. Press the seam allowances toward the A Blocks. <u>At this point each block row should measure 10-1/2 x 70-1/2-inches.</u>

Block row for left side

Block row for right side

Piecing - Block C, makes 8 blocks

Step 1 Aligning long edges, sew together one of the 4-1/2 x 44-inch **RED PRINT** strips and the 6-1/2 x 44-inch **GOLD PRINT** strip. Press the strip set referring to **Hints and Helps for Pressing Strip Sets**. Cut the strip set into segments.

Crosscut 8, 4-1/2-inch wide segments

Hints and Helps for Pressing Strip Sets

When sewing strips of fabric together for strip sets, it is important to press the seam allowances nice and flat, usually to the dark fabric.

avoid this rainbow effect

Be careful not to stretch as you press, causing a "rainbow effect." This will affect the accuracy and shape of the pieces cut from the strip set. Press on the wrong side first with the strips perpendicular to the ironing board. Flip the piece over and press on the right side to prevent little pleats from forming at the seams. Laying the strip set lengthwise on the ironing board seems to encourage the rainbow effect.

Step 2 Sew the Step 1 segments to the 6-1/2 x 10-1/2-inch **BEIGE/GREEN LEAF PRINT** rectangles; press. <u>At this point each Block C should measure 10-1/2-inches squares.</u>

Block C, make 4 for left side

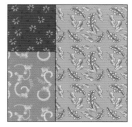

Block C, make 4 for right side

Piecing - Block D, makes 6 blocks

Step 1 Aligning long edges, sew together one of the 4-1/2 x 44-inch **RED PRINT** strips and the 6-1/2 x 44-inch **BEIGE DOT** strip; press. Cut the strip set into segments.

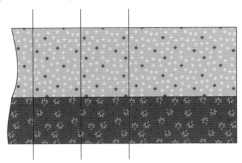

Crosscut 6, 4-1/2-inch wide segments

Step 2 Sew the Step 1 segments to the 6-1/2 x 10-1/2-inch **SMALL RED/ GREEN FLORAL** rectangles; press. <u>At this point each Block D should measure 10-1/2-inches square.</u>

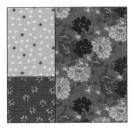

Block D,
make 3 for left side

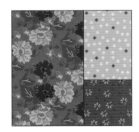

Block D,
make 3 for right side

Step 3 Referring to the diagrams for block placement, sew together 4 of the C Blocks and the 3 D Blocks in 2 vertical block rows. Press the seam allowances toward the C Blocks. <u>At this point each block row should measure 10-1/2 x 70-1/2-inches.</u>

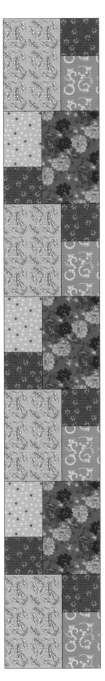

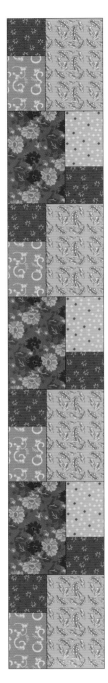

Block row for left side   Block row for right side

Piecing - Block E, makes 3 blocks

Step 1 Sew 3 of the 2-1/2 x 10-1/2-inch **RED PRINT** rectangles to the bottom edges of the 8-1/2 x 10-1/2-inch **RED/CREAM FLORAL** rectangles; press. At this point each Block E should measure 10-1/2-inches square.

Block E, make 3

Step 2 Referring to the diagram for block placement, sew together 4 of the A Blocks and the 3 E Blocks in a vertical block row. Press the seam allowances toward the E Blocks. At this point the block row should measure 10-1/2 x 70-1/2-inches.

Block row for center

Quilt Center Assembly

Referring to the quilt center assembly diagram for block placement, sew the block rows together to make the quilt center; press. At this point the quilt center should measure 50-1/2 x 70-1/2-inches.

Quilt Center Assembly Diagram

Borders

*Note: The yardage given allows for the **LARGE RED FLORAL** wide outer border strips to be cut on the lengthwise grain (a couple extra inches are allowed for trimming). Cutting the wide border strips lengthwise will eliminate the need for piecing. The yardage given allows for the inner and middle border strips to be cut on the crosswise grain. Diagonally piece the strips as needed referring to **Diagonal Piecing** instructions on page 75. Read through **Border** instructions on page 73 for general instructions on adding borders.*

Cutting

From **BEIGE DOT**:
- Cut 7, 2-1/2 x 44-inch inner border strips

From **RED/CREAM FLORAL**:
- Cut 7, 6-1/2 x 44-inch wide middle border strips

From **GOLD PRINT**:
- Cut 1, 6-1/2 x 44-inch strip. From the strip cut:
  4, 6-1/2-inch corner squares

From **OLIVE GREEN FLORAL**:
- Cut 9, 2-1/2 x 44-inch narrow middle border strips

From **LARGE RED FLORAL**:
- Cut 2, 10-1/2 x 112-inch side outer border strips
  (cut on the lengthwise grain)
- Cut 2, 10-1/2 x 75-inch top/bottom outer border
  strips (cut on the lengthwise grain)

Attaching the Borders

Step 1 Attach the 2-1/2-inch wide **BEIGE DOT** inner border strips.

Step 2 Attach the 6-1/2-inch wide **RED/CREAM FLORAL** top/bottom middle border strips.

Step 3 For the side borders, measure the quilt from top to bottom through the middle including the seam allowances, but not the borders just added. Cut the 6-1/2-inch wide **RED/CREAM FLORAL** side border strips to this length. Sew a 6-1/2-inch **GOLD PRINT** corner square to both ends of the side border strips; press. Sew the borders to the side edges of the quilt; press.

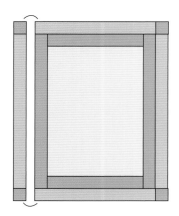

Step 4 Attach the 2-1/2-inch wide **OLIVE GREEN** narrow middle border strips.

Step 5 Attach the 10-1/2-inch wide **LARGE RED FLORAL** outer border strips.

Putting It All Together

Cut the 8 yard length of backing fabric in thirds crosswise to make 3, 2-2/3 yard lengths. Refer to **Finishing the Quilt** on page 75 for complete instructions.

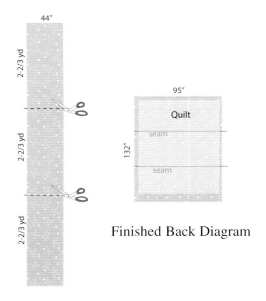

Finished Back Diagram

Quilting Suggestions:
- Quilt center - horizontal rows of **TB38 Pansy Vine**.
- **BEIGE DOT** inner border - 2-inch channel stitching.
- **RED/CREAM FLORAL** wide middle border - **TB37 Pansy Vine**.
- **GOLD PRINT** corner squares - **TB6 Leaf Quartet**.
- **OLIVE GREEN FLORAL** narrow middle border - 2-inch channel stitching.
- **LARGE RED FLORAL** outer border - 2-inch wide crosshatching.

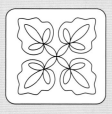

TB 6 Leaf Quartet (5")

TB 38 Pansy Vine (7")

THIMBLEBERRIES® quilt stencils by Quilting Creations International are available at your local quilt shop.

Binding

Cutting

From **OLIVE GREEN FLORAL**:
• Cut 10 to 11, 2-3/4 x 44-inch strips

Sew the binding to the quilt using a 3/8-inch seam allowance. This measurement will produce a 1/2-inch wide finished double binding. Refer to **Binding** and **Diagonal Piecing** on page 75 for complete instructions.

Sunsplashed
90 x 110-inches

Sunsplashed

2nd Color Option

90 x 110-inches

abrics and Supplies

4-1/8 yards **BLACK/BROWN PRINT** for pieced blocks and outer border
(cut on the lengthwise grain)

2/3 yard **BROWN PRINT** for pieced blocks

1 yard **RED PRINT** for pieced blocks and narrow middle border

2-1/8 yards **GOLD FLORAL** for pieced blocks and wide middle border

1/2 yard **GOLD/RED PRINT** for pieced blocks and corner squares

1/2 yard **GOLD PRINT** for pieced blocks

3/4 yard **BLUE PRINT** for pieced blocks and inner border

1/2 yard **BLUE/GOLD LEAF** for pieced blocks

1 yard **RED PRINT** for binding

8 yards **BEIGE PRINT** for backing

quilt batting, at least 96 x 116 -inches

Before beginning this project, read through General Instructions on page 62.

Plain and Simple Pillow

18-inches square

Fabric and Supplies
for one pillow

1-1/4 yards **PRINT** for pillow top and backing
18-inch square pillow form

Before beginning this project, read through
General Instructions on page 62.

Assembling the Pillow

Cutting

From **PRINT**:
- Cut 1, 18-1/2-inch square for pillow top
- Cut 1, 24 x 44-inch strip. From the strip cut:
    2, 18-1/2 x 24-inch pillow back rectangles

Assembling the Pillow Back

Step 1 With wrong sides together, fold each
18-1/2 x 24-inch **PRINT** pillow back rectangle in
half crosswise to make 2, 12 x 18-1/2-inch double-thick
pillow back pieces. Overlap the 2 folded edges so the
pillow back measures 18-1/2-inches square. Pin the
pieces together and machine baste around the entire piece
to create a single pillow back, using a 1/4-inch seam
allowance. The double thickness of the pillow back will
make it more stable and give it a nice finishing touch.

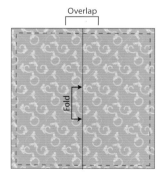

Make 1

Step 2 With right sides together, layer the pillow
back and the pillow top; pin. Stitch around the outside
edges using a 3/8-inch seam allowance. Turn the pillow
right side out and insert the pillow form through the
back opening.

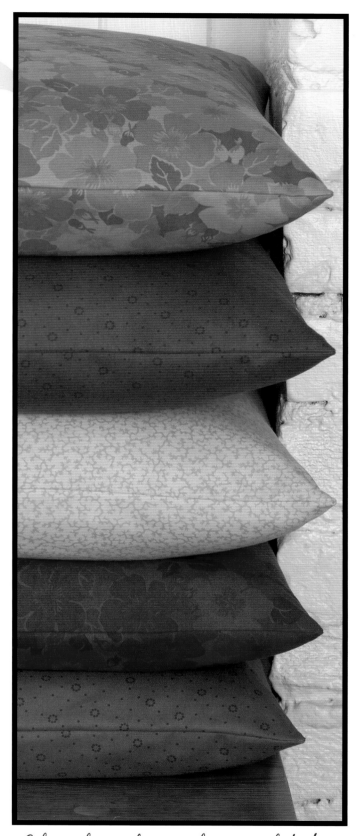

Color, color, and more color – simple knife edge pillows can add lots of pizazz to every room in your house.

Chenille Bath Rug

24 x 35-inches

Fabrics and Supplies

DO NOT PREWASH FABRICS

3-1/8 yards* **LARGE BLUE FLORAL** for top (4 layers of fabric)

7/8 yard **GOLD PRINT** for backing

3/4 yard **PLUM PRINT** for binding

lightweight cotton batting, at least 28 x 39-inches
(follow batting manufacturer's instructions concerning prewashing)

scissors, marking pencil, water spray bottle

temporary fabric adhesive, chenille brush

rotary cutter, mat, and wide clear plastic ruler with 1/8-inch markings
and 45° angle lines

walking foot - (since you are stitching on the bias,
the use of an even-feed walking foot is highly recommended)

Before beginning this project, read through General Instructions on page 62.

Bath Rug

Cutting

From **LARGE BLUE FLORAL**:

- Determine the repeat of your fabric, then cut:
    - 1, 29 x 40-inch rectangle for the base layer
    - 3, 28 x 39-inch rectangles for the "chenille" layers

Note: The "base" layer is a bit larger than the top 3 layers to make it easier to locate when you begin cutting the "chenille" layers. <u>*You should not cut the base layer, GOLD backing layer, or batting.*</u>

From **GOLD PRINT**:

- Cut 1, 28 x 39-inch rectangle for backing

Bath Rug Assembly

Step 1 Iron all the fabrics with a dry iron to remove wrinkles.

Step 2 Mark the <u>right side</u> of one of the 26 x 37-inch **LARGE BLUE FLORAL** rectangles. This will be your top layer. To do this, draw parallel diagonal lines 6-inches apart across the <u>right side</u> of the top layer using the 45° angle on your clear plastic ruler as a guide. The parallel lines are reference points to insure you keep a 45° angle when stitching at 1/2-inch intervals. Set this top layer aside.

Step 3 Now it is time to layer and adhere your fabrics together. Referring to manufacturer's instructions for complete directions, work on a flat protected surface. We suggest laying a bed sheet on the flat surface to protect your surface against overspray. With the <u>wrong side</u> of the **GOLD** backing facing up, pin the edges to the protective sheet to stabilize it.

Step 4 The next step is to adhere the batting to the <u>wrong side</u> of your **GOLD** backing fabric. To do this, lightly spray temporary fabric adhesive on the wrong side of the **GOLD** fabric.

Step 5 Position the batting on the **GOLD** rectangle; pat in place. Lightly spray the fabric adhesive on the batting. Position one of the <u>unmarked</u> **LARGE BLUE FLORAL** rectangles on the batting <u>right side up</u>. Pat in place and lightly spray.

Step 6 Carefully layer the remaining 2 <u>unmarked</u> **LARGE BLUE FLORAL** rectangles; (one at a time with the right side facing up) matching the "repeats." Lightly spray fabric adhesive on the right side of each layer. Match the repeats perfectly and pat each layer in place as you go.

Step 7 Next, layer the <u>marked</u> **LARGE BLUE FLORAL** rectangle, matching the repeats; pat in place.

Step 8 You will be stitching on the marked **LARGE BLUE FLORAL** top layer. Your parallel stitching lines will be placed 1/2-inch apart. First find your 1/2-inch seam allowance, then find a reference point on your walking foot to follow (it could be the outside edge on the right-hand side of the walking foot). This will help to insure accurate spacing while stitching. Check your spacing and 45° angle often (refer to your marked lines) to insure accuracy. Use a regular stitch length.

Note: The first stitching line should be through the center of the rectangle, then stitch on either side of the center line. As you stitch, keep in mind that you will need to turn your fabric after each line stitched and stitch in the opposite direction per row to keep from stretching your rug out of shape. Continue stitching parallel lines 1/2-inch apart over the entire surface of the rug.

Step 9 After all diagonal lines have been stitched, it is time to cut between the stitching lines using a sharp scissors. **Carefully cut between the lines of stitching through the 3 top fabric layers only**, leaving the **GOLD** backing, batting, and **LARGE BLUE FLORAL** base layer uncut.

Step 10 Now it is time to "chenille" your rug. Spray water on the rug to wet the cut edges of the fabric. Using the chenille brush, gently brush the edges of the cut strips to roughen them up. This is a messy job so you may want to do this outside. The cut edges should be frayed. Shake the rug well to remove more of the threads. Let the rug dry completely.

Step 11 Trim the layers of the bath rug so they are "square."

Binding

Cutting

From **PLUM PRINT**:

- Cut 4, 6-1/2 x 42-inch strips

Sew the binding to the bath rug using a scant 1-inch seam allowance. This measurement will produce a 1-inch wide finished double binding. Refer to **Binding** and **Diagonal Piecing** instructions on page 75.

Sunkissed Flowers

30 x 38-inches

Graphic floral appliqué and checkerboard pair beautifully with large border print for a stunning piece of artwork.

Sunkissed Flowers

30 x 38-inches

Fabrics and Supplies

1/4 yard **BEIGE DOT** for appliqué foundation rectangles

1/2 yard **RED PRINT** for checkerboard, lattice post squares,
and flower appliqués

1/4 yard **CREAM FLORAL** for checkerboard

1/4 yard **SMALL RED/GREEN FLORAL** for lattice segments
and flower appliqués

1/3 yard **OLIVE GREEN FLORAL** for inner border and
leaf/stem appliqués

1/8 yard **GOLD PRINT** for leaf appliqués

5/8 yard **BEIGE/GREEN LEAF PRINT** for outer border

3/8 yard **RED PRINT** for binding

1 yard **BEIGE/GREEN LEAF PRINT** for backing

quilt batting, at least 36 x 44-inches

pearl cotton or machine-embroidery thread for decorative stitches: black

paper-backed fusible web

tear-away fabric stabilizer for appliqué (optional)

Before beginning this project, read through General Instructions on page 62.

Fusible Web Appliqué Method

Cutting

From **BEIGE DOT**:
- Cut 1, 7-1/2 x 44-inch strip. From the strip cut:
  4, 7-1/2 x 8-1/2-inch appliqué foundation rectangles

Prepare the Appliqués

Step 1 Position the fusible web, paper side up, over the appliqué shapes on page 33. Trace the shapes onto fusible web the number of times indicated on the pattern pieces, leaving a small margin between each shape. Cut the shapes apart.

Note: When you are fusing a large shape, like the leaf, fuse just the outer edges of the shape so that it will not look stiff when finished. To do this, draw a line about 3/8-inch inside the leaf, and cut away the fusible web on this line.

Step 2 Following the manufacturer's instructions, fuse the shapes to the wrong side of the fabric chosen for the appliqués. Let the fabric cool and cut along the traced line. Peel away the paper backing from the fusible web.

Step 3 Referring to the block diagram, position the shapes on the 7-1/2 x 8-1/2-inch **BEIGE DOT** rectangles layering them as shown. *Note: The **GOLD PRINT** leaf will be fused and appliquéd in place after the quilt center is constructed.* Fuse the other shapes in place.

Step 4 We machine blanket stitched around the shapes using black machine embroidery thread. If you like, you could hand blanket stitch around the shapes with pearl cotton.

Note: We suggest pinning a rectangle of tear-away stabilizer to the backside of the block to be appliquéd so that it will lay flat when the machine appliqué is complete. We use the extra-lightweight Easy Tear™ sheets as a stabilizer. When the appliqué is complete, tear away the stabilizer.

Checkerboard Units

Makes 4 units

Cutting

From **RED PRINT**:
- Cut 3, 1-1/2 x 44-inch strips. From the strips cut:
  2, 1-1/2 x 26-inch strips
  1, 1-1/2 x 20-inch strip

From **CREAM FLORAL**:
- Cut 3, 1-1/2 x 44-inch strips. From the strips cut:
  1, 1-1/2 x 26-inch strip
  2, 1-1/2 x 20-inch strips

Piecing

Step 1 Aligning long edges, sew 1-1/2 x 26-inch **RED** strips to both side edges of the 1-1/2 x 26-inch **CREAM FLORAL** strip. Press the seam allowances toward the **RED** strips referring to **Hints and Helps for Pressing Strip Sets** on page 38. Cut the strip set into segments.

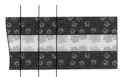

Crosscut 16, 1-1/2-inch wide segments

Step 2 Aligning long edges, sew 1-1/2 x 20-inch **CREAM FLORAL** strips to both side edges of the 1-1/2 x 20-inch **RED** strip. Press the seam allowances toward the **RED** strip. Cut the strip set into segments.

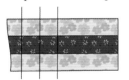

Crosscut 12, 1-1/2-inch wide segments

Step 3 Sew together 4 of the Step 1 segments and 3 of the Step 2 segments to make a checkerboard unit; press. At this point each checkerboard unit should measure 3-1/2 x 7-1/2-inches.

Make 4

Step 4 Sew the checkerboard units to the bottom edge of the appliquéd blocks; press. <u>At this point each flower block should measure 7-1/2 x 11-1/2-inches.</u>

Quilt Center

Cutting

From **SMALL RED/GREEN FLORAL**:
- Cut 3, 1-1/2 x 44-inch strips. From the strips cut:
    6, 1-1/2 x 11-1/2-inch lattice segments
    6, 1-1/2 x 7-1/2-inch lattice segments

From **RED PRINT**:
- Cut 3, 1-1/2 x 44-inch strips.
    From one of the strips cut:
    9, 1-1/2-inch lattice post squares

From **CREAM FLORAL**:
- Cut 2, 1-1/2 x 44-inch strips

Piecing and Quilt Center Assembly

Step 1 Referring to the quilt diagram, sew together 2 of the appliquéd blocks and 3 of the 1-1/2 x 11-1/2-inch **SMALL RED/GREEN FLORAL** lattice segments. Press the seam allowances toward the lattice segments. Make 2 block rows. <u>At this point each block row should measure 11-1/2 x 17-1/2-inches.</u>

Step 2 Sew together 2 of the 1-1/2 x 7-1/2-inch **SMALL RED/GREEN FLORAL** lattice segments and 3 of the 1-1/2-inch **RED** lattice posts. Press the seam allowances toward the lattice segments. Make 3 lattice strips. <u>At this point each lattice strip should measure 1-1/2 x 17-1/2-inches.</u>

Step 3 Referring to the quilt diagram, sew together the block rows and the lattice strips; press. <u>At this point the quilt center should measure 17-1/2 x 25-1/2-inches.</u>

Step 4 Aligning long edges, sew together the 1-1/2 x 44-inch **RED** and **CREAM FLORAL** strips in pairs. Press the seam allowances toward the **RED** strips. Cut the strip sets into segments.

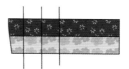

Crosscut 46, 1-1/2-inch wide segments

Step 5 For the top/bottom checkerboard borders, sew together 9 of the Step 4 segments. Remove a **RED** square from the end of the strip; press. Make 2 strips. <u>At this point each checkerboard border should measure 1-1/2 x 17-1/2-inches.</u> Sew the checkerboard borders to the top/bottom edges of the quilt center; press.

Make 2

Step 6 For the side checkerboard borders, sew together 14 of the Step 4 segments. Remove a **CREAM FLORAL** square from the end of the strip; press. Make 2 strips. <u>At this point each checkerboard border should measure 1-1/2 x 27-1/2-inches.</u> Sew the checkerboard borders to the side edges of the quilt center; press. <u>At this point the quilt center should measure 19-1/2 x 27-1/2-inches.</u>

Step 7 The remaining **GOLD** leaves can be fused and appliquéd to the quilt center at this time.

Borders

*Note: The yardage given allows for the border strips to be cut on the crosswise grain. Read through **Border** instructions on page 73 for general instructions on adding borders.*

Cutting

From **OLIVE GREEN FLORAL**:
- Cut 3, 1 x 44-inch inner border strips

From **BEIGE/GREEN LEAF PRINT**:
- Cut 3, 5-1/2 x 44-inch outer border strips

Attaching the Borders

Step 1 Attach the 1-inch wide **OLIVE GREEN FLORAL** inner border strips.

Step 2 Attach the 5-1/2-inch wide **BEIGE/GREEN LEAF PRINT** outer border strips.

Putting It All Together

Trim the backing and batting so they are approximately 6-inches larger than the quilt top. Refer to **Finishing the Quilt** on page 75 for complete instructions.

Quilting Suggestions:

- Appliqué shapes - outline stitch around each shape
- **BEIGE DOT** background - small meander
- **CREAM FLORAL** checkerboard - small meander
- Lattice, **RED** checkerboard, and **GREEN** inner border - no quilting
- **BEIGE/GREEN LEAF** outer border - **TB31 Blossom Swirl**

THIMBLEBERRIES® quilt stencils by Quilting Creations International are available at your local quilt shop.

Binding

From **RED PRINT**:
- Cut 4, 2-3/4 x 44-inch strips

Sew the binding to the quilt using a 3/8-inch seam allowance. This measurement will produce a 1/2-inch wide finished double binding. Refer to **Binding** and **Diagonal Piecing** on page 75 for complete instructions.

TB 31 Blossom Swirl (3")

Sunkissed Flowers
30 x 38-inches

Placement Diagram

Outer Flower

Trace 4 onto fusible web
Red

Flower Center

Trace 4
onto fusible web
Red

Stem
Trace 4 onto fusible web
Green

Sunkissed Flowers

Appliqué Shapes

Leaf

Trace 12
onto fusible web

8 - Green
4 - Gold

Middle Flower

Trace 4
onto fusible web
Small Red/Green Floral

33

Drawstring Quilt Bag

20 x 33-inches

Fabric and Supplies

1-1/4 yards **PRINT** for quilt bag

1-1/2 yards twill tape for tie

seam ripper and safety pin

Before beginning this project, read through
General Instructions on page 62.

Assembling The Quilt Bag

Cutting

From **PRINT**:

• Cut 1, 40-inch square for quilt bag

Step 1 Referring to the Step 2 diagram, with right sides together, fold the square in half and sew the bottom and side raw edges together using a 3/8-inch seam allowance; press.

Pillowcases and quilt storage bags all in one! Simply add twill tape, roll up a quilt and store safely or use as an accessory.

Step 2 Turn the open edge under 1/2-inch; press. Turn the same edge under 6-inches; press. Topstitch the folded edge in place to make a large casing.

Turn under 1/2-inch

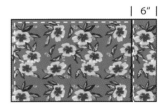

| 6" |

Step 3 Using a seam ripper, carefully remove a few stitches (about 1-inch in length) from the inside side seam. This opening is for inserting the twill tape. Hand tack the edges of the opening to secure them. Pin the end of the twill tape to the safety pin and insert it into the small opening. Thread the twill tape through the large casing. Turn the bag right side out; press.

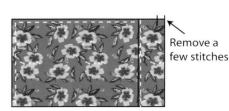

Remove a few stitches

Step 4 Roll up your quilt so it will fit into the quilt bag. Insert the quilt into the quilt bag and pull the drawstring tight; tie.

Note: *This bag can be used as a pillowcase omitting the drawstring.*

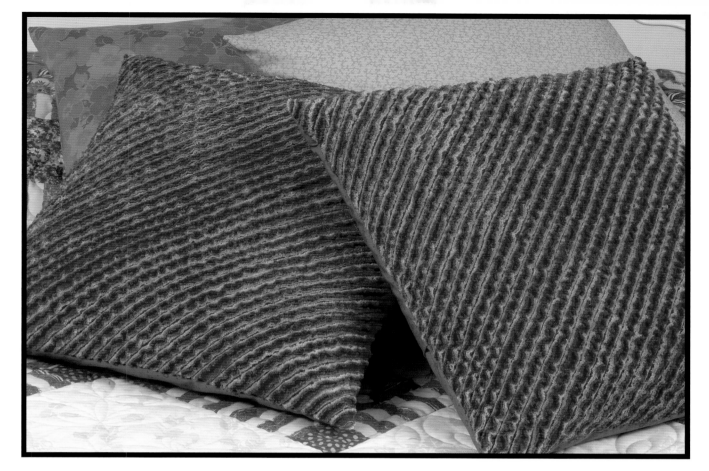

Chenille Pillow

18-inches square

Fabrics and Supplies

for one pillow   *DO NOT PREWASH FABRICS*

20-inch square **RASPBERRY FLORAL** for top layer
20-inch square **OLIVE GREEN FLORAL** for second layer
20-inch square **GOLD PRINT** for third layer
20-inch square **DARK ROSE PRINT** for fourth layer
1-1/3 yards **DARK GREEN PRINT** for base layer and backing
18-inch pillow form
scissors, marking pencil, water spray bottle
temporary fabric adhesive, chenille brush
rotary cutter, mat, and wide clear plastic ruler with 1/8-inch
markings and 45° angle lines
walking foot - (since you are stitching on the bias, the use of an
even-feed walking foot is highly recommended)

Before beginning this project, read through
General Instructions on page 62.

Pillow Top

Cutting

From **RASPBERRY FLORAL, OLIVE GREEN FLORAL, GOLD PRINT,** and **DARK ROSE PRINT**:
• Cut 1, 20-inch square from *each* fabric

From **DARK GREEN PRINT**:
• Cut 1, 22-inch square for base layer

Assembling the Pillow Top

Step 1 Mark the <u>right side</u> of the 20-inch **RASPBERRY FLORAL** top layer square. To do this, draw parallel diagonal lines 6-inches apart across the <u>right side</u> of the top layer using the 45° angle on your clear plastic ruler as a guide. The parallel lines are reference points to insure you keep a 45° angle when stitching at 1/2-inch intervals.

Step 2 The next step is to adhere your fabrics together. To do this, lightly spray temporary fabric adhesive on the <u>top side</u> of the 22-inch **DARK GREEN** base layer square (refer to manufacturer's instructions). This base square is larger than the other top layers to make it easier to cut the top 4 layers.

Step 3 Position the **DARK ROSE** fourth layer on the base layer. Lightly spray adhesive on the right side of the **DARK ROSE** layer. Adhere the remaining layers in this manner. <u>Do not spray the **RASPBERRY FLORAL** top marked layer.</u> Pat each layer in place as you go.

Step 4 You will be stitching on the **RASPBERRY FLORAL** top layer. Your parallel stitching lines will be placed 1/2-inch apart. First find your 1/2-inch seam allowance, then find a reference point on your walking foot to follow. This will help to insure accurate spacing while stitching. Use a regular stitch length.

Note: The first stitching line should be through the center of the square, then stitch on either side of the center line. As you stitch, keep in mind that you will need to turn your fabric after each line stitched and stitch in the opposite direction per row to keep from stretching your square out of shape. Continue stitching parallel lines 1/2-inch apart over the entire surface.

Step 5 After all diagonal lines have been stitched, it is time to cut between the stitching lines using a sharp scissors. Lay the stitched square on a flat surface and hold on to the edge of the **DARK GREEN** base layer. **Carefully cut between the lines of stitching through the top 4 fabric layers only**, leaving the **DARK GREEN** base layer uncut.

Step 6 Now it is time to "chenille" your pillow top. Spray water on the pillow top to wet the cut edges of the fabric. Using the chenille brush, gently brush the edges of the cut strips to roughen them up. This is a messy job so you may want to do this outside. The cut edges should be frayed. Shake the pillow top well to remove more of the threads. Let the pillow top dry completely.

Step 7 Trim the pillow top so it is 18-1/2-inches square.

Pillow Back

From **DARK GREEN PRINT**:
- Cut 1, 24 x 44-inch strip. From the strip cut:
  2, 18-1/2 x 24-inch pillow back rectangles

Assembling the Pillow Back

Step 1 With wrong sides together, fold each **DARK GREEN PRINT** pillow back rectangle in half crosswise to make 2, 12 x 18-1/2-inch double-thick pillow back pieces. Overlap the 2 folded edges so the pillow back measures 18-1/2-inches square. Pin the pieces together and machine baste around the entire piece to create a single pillow back, using a 1/4-inch seam allowance. The double thickness of the pillow back will make it more stable and give it a nice finishing touch.

Make 1

Step 2 With right sides together, layer the pillow back and the pillow top; pin. Stitch around the outside edges using a 3/8-inch seam allowance. Turn the pillow right side out and insert the pillow form through the back opening.

PAINT PALETTE

BROOKSIDE MOSS

GOLDEN STRAW

DESERT TAN

POTTERY RED

GOLDEN TAN

Paint chips from the Benjamin Moore® Collection

Checkerboard Pillow Sham

20 x 26-inches

Fabrics and Supplies

for 1 pillow sham

1/2 yard **LARGE BLUE FLORAL** for pieced pillow top

1/2 yard **CREAM FLORAL** for pieced pillow top

2-1/2 yards **PLUM STRIPE** for ruffle and pillow backing

quilt batting, at least 24 x 30-inches

24 x 30-inch rectangle **BEIGE** for lining pillow top

20 x 26-inch pillow form

Before beginning this project, read through General Instructions on page 62.

Checkerboard Pillow Top

Cutting

From **LARGE BLUE FLORAL**:
• Cut 5, 2-1/2 x 44-inch strips

From **CREAM FLORAL**:
• Cut 5, 2-1/2 x 44-inch strips

Piecing

Step 1 Aligning long raw edges, sew together 3 of the 2-1/2 x 44-inch **LARGE BLUE FLORAL** strips and 2 of the 2-1/2 x 44-inch **CREAM FLORAL** strips. Press the seam allowances toward the **LARGE BLUE FLORAL** strips referring to **Hints and Helps for Pressing Strip Sets** on page 38. Cut the strip set into segments.

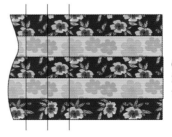

Crosscut 13, 2-1/2-inch wide segments

Step 2 Aligning long raw edges, sew together 2 of the 2-1/2 x 44-inch **LARGE BLUE FLORAL** strips and 3 of the 2-1/2 x 44-inch **CREAM FLORAL** strips; press. Cut the strip set into segments.

Crosscut 13,
2-1/2-inch wide segments

Step 3 Referring to the diagram for placement, sew together 7 of the Step 1 segments and 6 of the Step 2 segments; press. At this point the upper checkerboard unit should measure 10-1/2 x 26-1/2-inches.

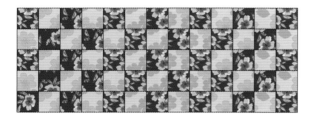

Step 4 Referring to the diagram for placement, sew together 6 of the Step 1 segments and 7 of the Step 2 segments; press. At this point the lower checkerboard unit should measure 10-1/2 x 26-1/2-inches.

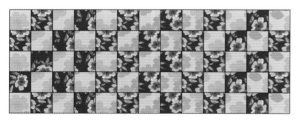

Step 5 Referring to the diagram, sew the Step 3 checkerboard unit to the top edge of the Step 4 checkerboard unit; press. At this point the pillow top should measure 20-1/2 x 26-1/2-inches.

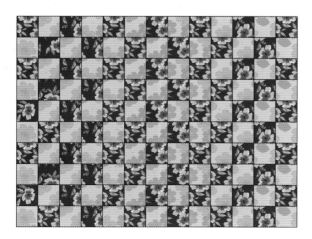

Hints and Helps for Pressing Strip Sets

When sewing strips of fabric together for strip sets, it is important to press the seam allowances nice and flat, usually to the dark fabric. Be careful not to stretch as you press, causing a "rainbow effect."

Avoid this rainbow effect

This will affect the accuracy and shape of the pieces cut from the strip set. Press on the wrong side first with the strips perpendicular to the ironing board. Flip the piece over and press on the right side to prevent little pleats from forming at the seams. Laying the strip set lengthwise on the ironing board seems to encourage the rainbow effect.

Quilting the Pillow Top

Step 1 Layer the checkerboard pillow top, the 24 x 30-inch quilt batting rectangle, and the **BEIGE** lining rectangle with right sides facing out. Hand baste (or spray baste) the layers together.

Step 2 Quilt the pillow top as desired. Our pillow top was machine quilted with an X in each **BEIGE** square. Trim the batting and backing even with the checkerboard pillow top. To prepare the pillow top before attaching the ruffle, I suggest hand basting the edges of the 3 layers together. This will prevent the edges of the pillow top from rippling when the ruffle is attached.

Pillow Ruffle

Cutting

From **PLUM STRIPE**:
- Cut 7, 6-1/2 x 44-inch strips

Attaching the Ruffle

Step 1 Piece the 6-1/2-inch wide **PLUM STRIPE** strips together on the straight of grain rather than on the diagonal (the stripes will be easier to match), to make a continuous ruffle strip (280-inches long).

Step 2 Fold the strip in half lengthwise, wrong sides together; press. Divide the ruffle strip into 4 equal segments; mark the quarter points with safety pins.

Step 3 To gather the ruffle, position quilting thread a scant 1/4-inch from the raw edges of the ruffle strip. You will need a length of thread 280-inches long. Secure one end of the thread by stitching across it. Zigzag stitch over the thread all the way around the ruffle strip, taking care not to sew through it.

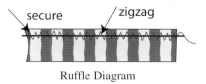

Ruffle Diagram

Step 4 Divide the edges of the pillow top into 4 equal segments; mark the quarter points with safety pins. With right sides together and raw edges aligned, pin the ruffle to the pillow top, matching the quarter points. Pull up the gathering stitches until the ruffle fits the pillow top, taking care to allow extra fullness in the ruffle at each corner. Sew the ruffle to the pillow front using a 3/8-inch seam allowance.

Pillow Back

Cutting

From **PLUM STRIPE**:
- Cut 2, 20-1/2 x 36-inch pillow back rectangles

Assembling the Pillow Back

Step 1 With wrong sides together, fold each **PLUM STRIPE** pillow back rectangle in half crosswise to make 2, 18 x 20-1/2-inch double-thick pillow back pieces. Overlap the 2 folded edges so the pillow back measures 20-1/2 x 26-1/2-inches. Pin the pieces together and machine baste around the entire piece to create a single pillow back using a 3/8-inch seam allowance. The double thickness of the pillow back will make it more stable and give it a nice finishing touch.

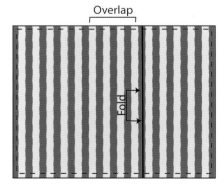

Step 2 With wrong sides together, layer the pillow back and the pillow top; pin. Stitch around the outside edges using a 1/2-inch seam allowance.

Step 3 Turn the pillow sham right side out and fluff up the ruffle. Insert the pillow form through the back opening.

Decorating . . .

Now it's time for fun -

Choosing paint colors that blend with colors used in fabric is an easy way to freshen up any room.

PAINT PALETTE

DUNMORE CREAM

SHADOW

SEA LIFE

GALAXY

Paint chips are from the Benjamin Moore® Collection

Shower Curtain

Personalize your bath with a stunning
pieced shower curtain.

Shower Curtain

72 x 74-inches

Lightweight polyester batting should be used as the batting. A cotton batting will be too heavy and will absorb humidity. Batting may also be eliminated.

Fabrics and Supplies

1-2/3 yards **PLUM STRIPE** for center rectangle

1-3/8 yards **LARGE BLUE FLORAL** for outer border

7/8 yard **GOLD PRINT** for inner border, top border, and corner squares

2/3 yard **SMALL BLUE/PLUM FLORAL** for middle border and pieced border

1/4 yard *each* of **5 ASSORTED PRINTS** for pieced border

2-1/2 yards **PLUM PRINT** for binding and ties

4-1/2 yards **GOLD PRINT** for backing

lightweight polyester quilt batting, at least 78 x 80-inches

Optional: 72-inch square shower curtain liner (with buttonholes, not eyelets) and buttons to secure liner to quilted shower curtain.

Before beginning this project, read through General Instructions on page 62.

Shower Curtain

Note: *The yardage given allows for the border strips to be cut on the crosswise grain. Diagonally piece the strips as needed, referring to **Diagonal Piecing** on page 75 for complete instructions. Read through **Border** instructions on page 73 for general instructions on adding borders.*

Cutting

From **PLUM STRIPE**:
• Cut 1, 42-1/2 x 57-1/2-inch rectangle

From **LARGE BLUE FLORAL**:
• Cut 6, 7-1/2 x 44-inch outer border strips

From **GOLD PRINT**:
• Cut 4, 1-1/2 x 44-inch inner border strips
• Cut 2, 7-1/2-inch corner squares
• Cut 2, 2-1/2 x 44-inch top border strips

From **SMALL BLUE/PLUM FLORAL**:
• Cut 6, 2-1/2 x 44-inch middle border strips
• Cut 2, 6-1/2-inch squares for pieced border

From *one* of the **ASSORTED PRINTS**:
• Cut 4, 6-1/2-inch squares for pieced border

From *each* of the **remaining 4 ASSORTED PRINTS**:
• Cut 6, 6-1/2-inch squares for pieced border
    (a total of 24 squares)

Attaching the Borders

Step 1 Attach the 1-1/2-inch wide **GOLD** inner border strips to the bottom and side edges of the 42-1/2 x 57-1/2-inch **PLUM STRIPE** rectangle.

Step 2 Attach the 2-1/2-inch wide **SMALL BLUE/PLUM FLORAL** middle border strips to the bottom and side edges of the Step 1 unit.

Step 3 Referring to the shower curtain diagram, sew together 8 of the 6-1/2-inch **ASSORTED PRINT** squares for the bottom border; press. <u>At this point the strip should measure 6-1/2 x 48-1/2-inches.</u> Sew the strip to the bottom edge of the shower curtain center; press.

Step 4 Referring to the shower curtain diagram for block placement, sew together 10 of the 6-1/2-inch **ASSORTED PRINT** squares; press. Make 2 strips for the side borders. Sew a 6-1/2-inch **SMALL BLUE/PLUM FLORAL** square to the bottom edge

of each strip; press. <u>At this point each strip should measure 6-1/2 x 66-1/2-inches.</u> Sew the strips to the side edges of the shower curtain center; press.

Step 5 Attach the 7-1/2-inch wide **LARGE BLUE FLORAL** bottom outer border strip.

Step 6 For the side borders, measure just the quilt including the seam allowances, but not the bottom border just added. Cut the 7-1/2-inch wide **LARGE BLUE FLORAL** side border strips to this length. Sew 7-1/2-inch **GOLD** corner squares to both ends of the border strips; press. Sew the strips to the side edges of the shower curtain; press.

Step 7 Attach the 2-1/2-inch wide **GOLD PRINT** top border strip to the shower curtain.

Putting It All Together

Cut the 4-1/2 yard length of backing fabric in half crosswise to make 2, 2-1/4 yard lengths. Refer to **Finishing the Quilt** on page 75 for complete instructions.

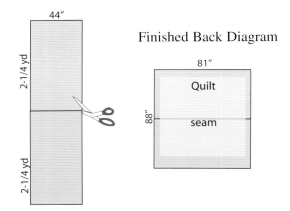

Quilting Suggestions:

• We suggest using a lightweight polyester batting so the shower curtain will not be too heavy. Quilt the shower curtain with a medium meander design.

Binding

Cutting

From **PLUM PRINT**:
- Cut 8, 6-1/2 x 44-inch strips

Attaching the Binding

Sew the binding to the shower curtain using a scant 1-inch seam allowance. This measurement will produce a 1-inch wide finished double binding. (The ties will be sewn to the backside of the shower curtain before the binding is hand stitched in place.) Refer to **Binding** and **Diagonal Piecing** instructions on page 75 for general instructions on adding borders.

Shower Curtain Ties

Cutting

From **PLUM PRINT**:
- Cut 8, 4 x 44-inch strips. From the strips cut: 24, 4 x 11-inch rectangles for ties

Attaching the Ties

Step 1 To finish the top edge of each 4 x 11-inch **PLUM** rectangle, fold under 1/4-inch on one short edge; press. With wrong sides together, fold the rectangle in half lengthwise so it is 2-inches wide; press. Unfold the rectangle and bring the raw edges to meet at the center fold line; press. Fold at the center fold line so the strip is 1-inch wide; press.

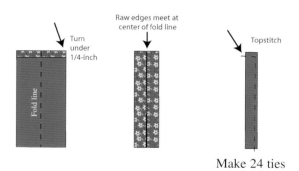

Make 24 ties

Step 2 Topstitch close to the folded top and side edges.

Step 3 At the top edge of the shower curtain, mark 12 evenly spaced positions for the ties.

Step 4 On the backside of the shower curtain, having the raw edges aligned, sew 2 ties at each position using a scant 1-inch seam allowance.

top raw edge

backside

Step 5 Turn the folded edge of the binding to the backside, over the raw edges of the ties and binding so the stitching line does not show. Hand sew the binding in place, folding in the mitered corners as you stitch.

Step 6 Flip each pair of ties up; pin in place. Hand stitch at both side edges of each pair of ties to secure them to the back of the shower curtain.

Optional: *To attach a shower curtain liner to the quilted shower curtain, position buttons on the backside of the quilted shower curtain so they line up with the buttonholes on the liner; sew in place. Button the liner in place.*

Step 7 Knot the ties around the shower curtain rod.

Shower Curtain
72 x 74-inches

Easy Does It Quilt

76 x 95-inches

. . . a contemporary quilt softens with lush prints.

Easy Does It Quilt

76 x 95-inches

abrics and Supplies

2-1/8 yards **SMALL RED/GREEN FLORAL** for quilt top
(cut on the lengthwise grain)

2-1/8 yards **RED/CREAM FLORAL** for quilt top
(cut on the lengthwise grain)

2-1/8 yards **LARGE RED FLORAL** for quilt top
(cut on the lengthwise grain)

3/4 yard **RED PRINT** for binding

5-3/4 yards **LARGE RED FLORAL** for backing

quilt batting, at least 82 x 101-inches

Before beginning this project, read through General Instructions on page 62.

Quilt Top

*The yardage given allows for the **SMALL RED/GREEN FLORAL, RED/CREAM FLORAL**, and **LARGE RED FLORAL** to be cut on the lengthwise grain (a couple extra inches are allowed for trimming). Cutting these strips lengthwise will eliminate the need for piecing.*

Cutting

From **SMALL RED/GREEN FLORAL**:
(cut on the lengthwise grain)
- Cut 3, 14 x 76-inch strips for quilt top

From **RED/CREAM FLORAL**:
(cut on the lengthwise grain)
- Cut 2, 14 x 76-inch strips for quilt top

From **LARGE RED FLORAL**:
(cut on the lengthwise grain)
- Cut 2, 14 x 76-inch strips for quilt top

Piecing

Step 1 Refer to the quilt top diagram for strip placement. Aligning long raw edges, sew together the 3, 14 x 76-inch **SMALL RED/GREEN FLORAL** strips, the 2, 14 x 76-inch **RED/CREAM FLORAL** strips, and the 2, 14 x 76-inch **LARGE RED FLORAL** strips.

Quilt Top Diagram

Step 2 Press the strips referring to **Hints and Helps for Pressing Strip Sets**. At this point the quilt top should measure 76 x 95-inches.

Hints and Helps for Pressing Strip Sets

When sewing strips of fabric together, it is important to press the seam allowances nice and flat, usually to the dark fabric. Be careful not to stretch as you press, causing a "rainbow effect." Press on the wrong side first with the strips perpendicular to the ironing board. Flip the piece over and press on the right side to prevent little pleats from forming at the seams. Laying the strip set lengthwise on the ironing board seems to encourage the rainbow effect.

Avoid this rainbow effect.

Putting It All Together

Cut the 5-3/4 yard length of backing fabric in half crosswise to make 2, 2-7/8 yard lengths. Refer to **Finishing the Quilt** on page 75 for complete instructions.

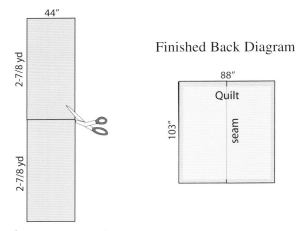

Finished Back Diagram

Quilting Suggestions:

- Vertical 4-inch wide channel stitching the length of the quilt

Binding

Cutting

From **RED PRINT**:
- Cut 9, 2-3/4 x 44-inch strips

Sew the binding to the quilt using a 3/8-inch seam allowance. This measurement will produce a 1/2-inch wide finished double binding. Refer to **Binding** and **Diagonal Piecing** on page 75 for complete instructions.

Making *your* House
A Home

Trim towels with fabric scraps to customize your bathroom accessories.

A simple knife edge pillow is a nice complement to a pieced sham with ruffle. The contrast makes both more outstanding.

Dust ruffles made from coordinatiog fabrics will automatically match your quilt.

Hint: "Store" other dust ruffles in layers on your bed.

Easy Does It Pillow Shams

20 x 29-inches

Easy, tailored pillow shams complement the bold pieces in the coordinating quilt.

abrics and Supplies for 2 pillow shams

2-5/8 yards **SMALL RED/GREEN FLORAL** for pillow tops and backings

1/2 yard **LARGE RED FLORAL** for pillow tops

1-1/8 yards **RED PRINT** for bindings

quilt batting, (2) pieces at least 24 x 32-inches

1-1/3 yards **BEIGE** for lining pillow tops

(2) 20 x 29-inch pillow forms

Before beginning this project, read through General Instructions on page 62.

Pillow Tops

Cutting

Note: The pillow sham strips should be cut on the crosswise grain.

From **SMALL RED/GREEN FLORAL**:
- Cut 3, 6-1/2 x 44-inch strips. From the strips cut:
  6, 6-1/2 x 20-1/2-inch strips

From **LARGE RED FLORAL**:
- Cut 2, 6-1/2 x 44-inch strips. From the strips cut:
  4, 6-1/2 x 20-1/2-inch strips

From **BEIGE**:
- Cut 2, 24 x 32-inch rectangles for lining the pillow top

Piecing

Aligning long raw edges, sew together 3 of the 6-1/2 x 20-1/2-inch **SMALL RED/GREEN FLORAL** strips and 2 of the 6-1/2 x 20-1/2-inch **LARGE RED FLORAL** strips; press. Make 2 pillow tops. <u>At this point each pillow top should measure 20-1/2 x 30-1/2-inches.</u>

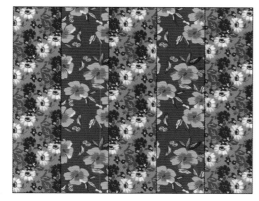

Make 2

Quilting The Pillow Tops

Step 1 Layer each pieced pillow top with a 24 x 32-inch quilt batting rectangle and a **BEIGE** lining rectangle with right sides facing out. Hand baste (or spray baste) the layers together.

Step 2 Quilt the pillow top as desired. Our pillow top was machine quilted with a 3-inch grid. Trim the batting and backing even with the pieced pillow top. To prepare the pillow top before attaching the binding, hand baste the edges of the 3 layers together. This will prevent the edges of the pillow top from rippling when the binding is attached.

Pillow Backs

Cutting

From **SMALL RED/GREEN FLORAL**:
- Cut 2, 36 x 44-inch strips. From the strips cut:
  4, 20-1/2 x 36-inch pillow back rectangles

Assembling the Pillow Back

Step 1 With wrong sides together, fold each **SMALL RED/GREEN FLORAL** pillow back rectangle in half crosswise to make 4, 18 x 20-1/2-inch double-thick pillow back pieces. To make one pillow back you will be using 2 of the rectangles. Overlap the 2 folded edges so the pillow back measures 20-1/2 x 29-1/2-inches. Pin the pieces together and machine baste around the entire piece to create a single pillow back, using a 3/8-inch seam allowance. The double thickness of the pillow back will make it more stable and give it a nice finishing touch.

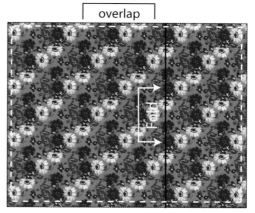

Make 2

Step 2 With wrong sides together, layer the pillow backs and the pillow tops in pairs; pin. Stitch around the outside edges using a 1/2-inch seam allowance.

Binding

From **RED PRINT**:
- Cut 6, 6-1/2 x 44-inch strips. Three strips will be used for each pillow sham. Sew the binding to the pillow shams using a scant 1-inch seam allowance. This measurement will produce a 1-inch wide finished double binding. Refer to **Binding** and **Diagonal Piecing** on page 75 for complete instructions.

4-Patch Pillow

18-inches square

. . . the perfect pillow, just plain or adorned with buttons.

Fabrics and Supplies

10 x 20-inch rectangle **RASPBERRY DOT** for pillow top

10 x 20-inch rectangle **RASPBERRY FLORAL** for pillow top

1/8 yard **CREAM PRINT** for pillow top bands

3/4 yard **RASPBERRY DOT** for pillow back

22-inch square **BEIGE PRINT** for pillow top lining

quilt batting, at least 22-inches square

18-inch square pillow form

13 buttons (optional)

Before beginning this project, read through General Instructions on page 62.

Pillow Top

Cutting

From **RASPBERRY DOT**:
- Cut 2, 9-inch squares

From **RASPBERRY FLORAL**:
- Cut 2, 9-inch squares

From **CREAM PRINT**:
- Cut 1, 1-1/2 x 44-inch strip. From the strip cut:
    1, 1-1/2 x 18-1/2-inch strip
    2, 1-1/2 x 9-inch strips

Piecing

Step 1 Sew one of the 9-inch **RASPBERRY DOT** squares and one of the **RASPBERRY FLORAL** squares to both side edges of a 1-1/2 x 9-inch **CREAM PRINT** strip; press. Make 2 units. <u>At this point each unit should measure 9 x 18-1/2-inches.</u>

Make 2

Step 2 Sew the Step 1 units to the top/bottom edges of the 1-1/2 x 18-1/2-inch **CREAM** strip; press. <u>At this point the pillow top should measure 18-1/2-inches square.</u>

Quilting Suggestions:

- Quilt a big X in each of the squares
- Quilt in-the-ditch along the sides of the **CREAM** bands

Pillow Assembly

Step 1 Layer the 22-inch **BEIGE** lining square batting, and pieced pillow top. Hand baste the layers together and quilt as desired. When quilting is complete, trim the excess **BEIGE** lining and batting even with the pillow top.

Step 2 Hand baste the edges together. This will prevent the edge of the pillow top from rippling when it is sewn to the pillow back.

Pillow Back

Cutting

From **RASPBERRY DOT**:
- Cut 1, 24 x 42-inch strip. From the strip cut:
    2, 18-1/2 x 24-inch pillow back rectangles

Assembling the Pillow Back

Step 1 With wrong sides together, fold each **RASPBERRY DOT** pillow back rectangle in half crosswise to make 2, 12 x 18-1/2-inch double-thick pillow back pieces. Overlap the 2 folded edges so the pillow back measures 18-1/2-inches square. Pin the pieces together and machine baste around the entire piece to create a single pillow back, using a 1/4-inch seam allowance. The double thickness of the pillow back will make it more stable and give it a nice finishing touch.

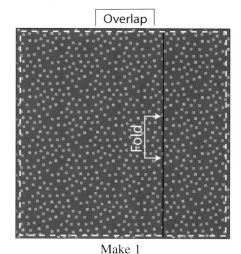

Make 1

Step 2 With right sides together, layer the pillow back and the pillow top; pin. Stitch around the outside edges using a 3/8-inch seam allowance. Turn the pillow right side out. If desired, sew buttons on the **CREAM** bands. Insert the pillow form through the back opening.

Simply Graphic
Queen

95 x 112-inche

A perfect bed quilt . . . includes a touch of tradition updated with graphic prints and fresh colors.

Simply Graphic Queen

95 x 112-inches

 Fabrics and Supplies

5-1/4 yards **LARGE GREEN FLORAL** for pieced blocks, middle border, and wide outer border (cut on the lengthwise grain)

2-1/2 yards **RASPBERRY STRIPE** for pieced blocks and narrow borders

3/8 yard **RASPBERRY DOT** for pieced blocks and corner squares

3/4 yard **CREAM FLORAL** for alternate blocks

1-1/8 yards **CREAM PRINT** for side and corner triangles

1 yard **SMALL ROSE/GREEN FLORAL** for second inner border

1 yard **RASPBERRY DOT** for binding

8-5/8 yards of 42-inch wide **CREAM FLORAL** for backing

OR

3-1/3 yards of 108-inch wide fabric for backing

quilt batting, at least 101 x 118-inches

Before beginning this project, read through General Instructions on page 62.

Pieced Blocks

Makes 12 blocks

*The yardage given allows for the **LARGE GREEN FLORAL** <u>wide outer border strips</u> to be cut on the lengthwise grain (a couple extra inches are allowed for trimming). Cutting these strips lengthwise will eliminate the need for piecing. The remaining pieces for the quilt should be cut on the crosswise grain.*

Cutting

From **LARGE GREEN FLORAL**:
- Cut a 3-1/4 yard piece (44 x 117-inches). Set aside to be used for the outer border, which will be cut on the lengthwise grain.
- From the remaining 2 yard piece cut:
  9, 4-1/2 x 44-inch middle border strips (cut on the crosswise grain; set aside to be used later).
  Also cut 3, 8-1/2 x 44-inch strips (cut on the crosswise grain).
  Then from these strips cut:
  12, 8-1/2-inch squares

From **RASPBERRY STRIPE**:
- Cut 10, 2-1/2 x 44-inch strips.
  From the strips cut:
  48, 2-1/2 x 8-1/2-inch rectangles

From **RASPBERRY DOT**:
- Cut 3, 2-1/2 x 44-inch strips.
  From the strip cut:
  48, 2-1/2-inch squares

Piecing

Step 1 Sew 2-1/2 x 8-1/2-inch **RASPBERRY STRIPE** rectangles to the top/bottom edges of the 8-1/2-inch **LARGE GREEN FLORAL** squares. Press the seam allowances toward the **RASPBERRY STRIPE** rectangles.

Make 12

Step 2 Sew 2-1/2-inch **RASPBERRY DOT** squares to both ends of the remaining 2-1/2 x 8-1/2-inch **RASPBERRY STRIPE** rectangles. Press the seam allowances toward the **RASPBERRY STRIPE** rectangles. Sew the units to the side edges of the Step 1 units; press. <u>At this point each pieced block should measure 12-1/2-inches square.</u>

Make 12

Quilt Center

Note: The side and corner triangles are larger than necessary and will be trimmed before the borders are added.

Cutting

From **CREAM FLORAL**:
- Cut 2, 12-1/2 x 44-inch strips. From the strips cut:
  6, 12-1/2-inch alternate blocks

From **CREAM PRINT**:
- Cut 2, 19 x 44-inch strips. From the strips cut:
  3, 19-inch squares. Cut the squares diagonally into quarters to make 12 triangles. You will be using only 10 for side triangles.

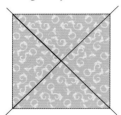

side triangles

Also cut 2, 11-inch squares. Cut the squares in half diagonally to make 4 corner triangles.

corner triangles

Quilt Center Assembly

Step 1 Referring to the quilt center assembly diagram for block placement, sew together the pieced blocks, the **CREAM FLORAL** alternate blocks, and the **CREAM PRINT** side triangles in 6 diagonal rows. Press the seam allowances toward the alternate blocks and side triangles.

Step 2 Pin the block rows together at the block intersections and sew together; press.

Step 3 Sew the **CREAM PRINT** corner triangles to the quilt center; press.

Step 4 Trim away the excess fabric from the side and corner triangles taking care to allow a 1/4-inch seam allowance beyond the corners of each block. Read through **Trimming Side and Corner Triangles** for complete instructions. <u>At this point the quilt center should measure approximately 51-1/2 x 68-1/2-inches.</u>

Quilt Center Assembly Diagram

Trimming Side and Corner Triangles

• Begin at a corner by lining up your ruler 1/4-inch beyond the points of the block corners as shown. Cut along the edge of the ruler. Repeat this procedure on all four sides of the quilt top.

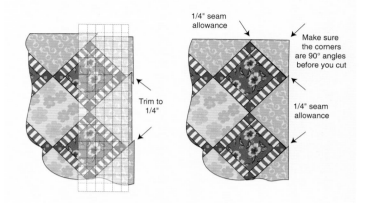

Borders

*Note: The yardage given allows for the **LARGE GREEN FLORAL** <u>wide outer border strips</u> to be cut on the lengthwise grain (a couple extra inches are allowed for trimming). Cutting the wide border strips lengthwise will eliminate the need for piecing. The yardage given allows for the <u>inner and middle border</u> strips to be cut on the crosswise grain. Diagonally piece the strips as needed referring to **Diagonal Piecing** instructions on page 75. Read through **Border** instructions on page 73 for general instructions on adding borders.*

Cutting

From **RASPBERRY STRIPE**:
• Cut 7, 2-1/2 x 44-inch inner border strips
• Cut 8, 2-1/2 x 44-inch middle border strips
• Cut 9, 2-1/2 x 44-inch narrow outer border strips

From **RASPBERRY DOT**:
• Cut 1, 2-1/2 x 44-inch strip. From the strip cut:
    12, 2-1/2-inch corner squares

From **SMALL ROSE/GREEN FLORAL**:
• Cut 7, 4-1/2 x 44-inch second inner border strips

From **LARGE GREEN FLORAL**:
The (9) 4-1/2-inch wide middle border strips were cut previously.

From the 3-1/4 yard of **LARGE GREEN FLORAL** fabric that was set aside earlier, cut:

    2, 8-1/2 x 117-inch side outer border strips
    (cut on the lengthwise grain)
    2, 8-1/2 x 83-inch top/bottom outer
    border strips (cut on the lengthwise grain)

Attaching the Borders

Step 1 Attach the 2-1/2-inch wide **RASPBERRY STRIPE** top/bottom inner border strips.

Step 2 For the side borders, measure the quilt from top to bottom through the middle including the seam allowances, but not the borders just added. Cut the 2-1/2-inch wide **RASPBERRY STRIPE** side inner border strips to this length. Sew a 2-1/2-inch **RASPBERRY DOT** corner square to both ends of the side border strips; press. Sew the borders to the side edges of the quilt; press.

Step 3 Attach the 4-1/2-inch wide **SMALL ROSE/ GREEN FLORAL** second inner border strips.

Step 4 Attach the 2-1/2-inch wide **RASPBERRY STRIPE** top/bottom middle border strips. Refer to Step 2 to attach the side borders with **RASPBERRY DOT** corner squares.

Step 5 Attach the 4-1/2-inch wide **LARGE GREEN FLORAL** middle border strips.

Step 6 Attach the 2-1/2-inch wide **RASPBERRY STRIPE** top/bottom narrow outer border strips. Refer to Step 2 to attach the side borders with **RASPBERRY DOT** corner squares.

Step 7 Attach the 8-1/2-inch wide **LARGE GREEN FLORAL** outer border strips.

Putting It All Together

- If you are using 108-inch wide backing fabric, simply trim the backing and batting so they are 3-inches larger on all 4 sides than the quilt top.

- If you are using 44-inch wide backing fabric, cut the 8-5/8 yard length of backing fabric in thirds cross-wise to make 3, 2-7/8 yard lengths.

- Refer to **Finishing the Quilt** on page 75 for complete instructions.

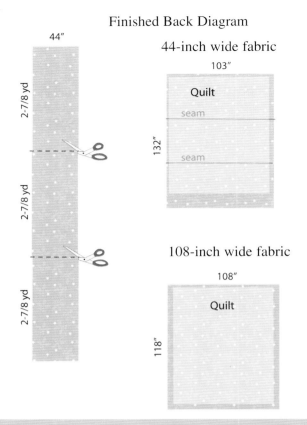

Finished Back Diagram

44"

2-7/8 yd

2-7/8 yd

2-7/8 yd

44-inch wide fabric

103"

Quilt

seam

132"

seam

108-inch wide fabric

108"

Quilt

118"

Quilting Suggestions:

- Pieced blocks - **TB8 Leaf Quartet**
- **CREAM FLORAL** alternate blocks - **TB18 Lady Slipper**
- **CREAM PRINT** side triangles - **TB39-12" Triangle Trail**
- **CREAM PRINT** corner triangles - **TB39-9" Triangle Trail**
- All borders - quilt as one border with meander design

THIMBLEBERRIES® quilt stencils by Quilting Creations International are available at your local quilt shop.

Binding

Cutting
From **RASPBERRY DOT**:
- Cut 11, 2-3/4 x 44-inch strips

Sew the binding to the quilt using a 3/8-inch seam allowance. This measurement will produce a 1/2-inch wide finished double binding. Refer to **Binding** and **Diagonal Piecing** on page 75 for complete instructions.

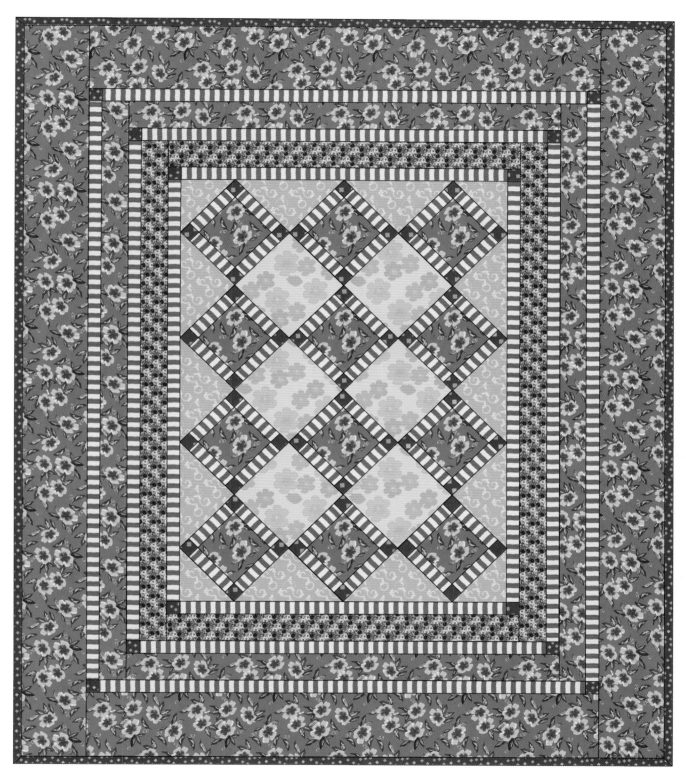

Simply Graphic Queen
95 x 112-inches

Simply Graphic Twin

75 x 92-inches

Sit awhile and dream of gardens to come.

Simply Graphic Twin

75 x 92-inches

Fabrics and Supplies

3-3/8 yards **BLUE/CREAM FLORAL** for pieced blocks and outer border
(cut on the lengthwise grain)

1-1/3 yards **GREEN PRINT** for pieced blocks and inner border

7/8 yard **BLUE PRINT** for pieced blocks, corner squares, and second middle border

3/4 yard **CREAM PRINT** for alternate blocks

1-1/8 yards **BEIGE FLORAL** for side and corner triangles

7/8 yard **BLUE PRINT** for binding

5-1/2 yards **SMALL BLUE/GREEN FLORAL** for backing

quilt batting, at least 81 x 98-inches

Before beginning this project, read through General Instructions on page 62.

---

*The yardage given allows for the **BLUE/CREAM FLORAL** <u>outer border strips</u> to be cut on the lengthwise grain (a couple extra inches are allowed for trimming). Cutting these strips lengthwise will eliminate the need for piecing. The remaining pieces for the quilt should be cut on the crosswise grain.*

Pieced Blocks

Makes 12 blocks

Cutting

From **BLUE/CREAM FLORAL**:
- Cut 3, 8-1/2 x 44-inch strips. From the strips cut: 12, 8-1/2-inch squares

From **GREEN PRINT**:
- Cut 10, 2-1/2 x 44-inch strips. From the strips cut: 48, 2-1/2 x 8-1/2-inch rectangles

From **BLUE PRINT**:
- Cut 3, 2-1/2 x 44-inch strips. From the strip cut: 48, 2-1/2-inch squares

Piecing

Step 1 Sew 2-1/2 x 8-1/2-inch **GREEN** rectangles to the top/bottom edges of the 8-1/2-inch **BLUE/CREAM FLORAL** squares. Press the seam allowances toward the **GREEN** rectangles.

Make 12

Step 2 Sew 2-1/2-inch **BLUE** squares to both ends of the remaining 2-1/2 x 8-1/2-inch **GREEN** rectangles. Press the seam allowances toward the **GREEN** rectangles. Sew the units to the side edges of the Step 1 units; press. <u>At this point each pieced block should measure 12-1/2-inches square.</u>

Make 12

Quilt Center

Note: The side and corner triangles are larger than necessary and will be trimmed before the borders are added.

Cutting

From **CREAM PRINT**:
- Cut 2, 12-1/2 x 44-inch strips. From the strips cut: 6, 12-1/2-inch alternate blocks

From **BEIGE FLORAL**:
- Cut 2, 19 x 44-inch strips. From the strips cut: 3, 19-inch squares. Cut the squares diagonally into quarters to make 12 triangles. You will be using only 10 for side triangles.

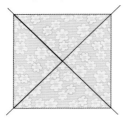 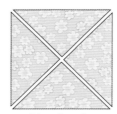

side triangles

Also cut 2, 11-inch squares. Cut the squares in half diagonally to make 4 corner triangles.

corner triangles

Quilt Center Assembly

Step 1 Referring to the quilt center assembly diagram for block placement, sew together the pieced blocks, the **CREAM** alternate blocks, and the **BEIGE FLORAL** side triangles in 6 diagonal rows. Press the seam allowances toward the alternate blocks and side triangles.

Step 2 Pin the block rows together at the block intersections and sew together; press.

Step 3 Sew the **BEIGE FLORAL** corner triangles to the quilt center; press.

Step 4 Trim away the excess fabric from the side and corner triangles taking care to allow a 1/4-inch seam allowance beyond the corners of each block. Read through **Trimming Side and Corner Triangles** on page 68 for complete instructions. At this point the quilt center should measure approximately 51-1/2 x 68-1/2-inches.

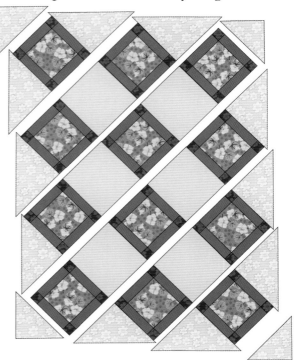

Borders

*Note: The yardage given allows for the **BLUE/CREAM FLORAL** first middle border and outer border strips to be cut on the lengthwise grain (a couple extra inches are allowed for trimming). Cutting the wide border strips lengthwise will eliminate the need for piecing. The yardage given allows for the **GREEN** inner border strips and the **BLUE** second middle border strips to be cut on the crosswise grain. Diagonally piece the strips as needed referring to **Diagonal Piecing** instructions on page 75. Read through **Border** instructions on page 73 for general instructions on adding borders.*

Cutting

From **GREEN PRINT**:
- Cut 7, 2-1/2 x 44-inch inner border strips

From **BLUE PRINT**:
- Cut 8, 2-1/2 x 44-inch second middle border strips
- Cut 8, 2-1/2-inch corner squares

From **BLUE/CREAM FLORAL**:
(cut on the lengthwise grain)
- Cut 2, 5-1/2 x 95-inch side outer border strips
- Cut 2, 5-1/2 x 68-inch top/bottom outer border strips
- Cut 2, 3-1/2 x 81-inch side first middle border strips
- Cut 2, 3-1/2 x 58-inch top/bottom first middle border strips

Attaching the Borders

Step 1 Attach the 2-1/2-inch wide **GREEN** top/bottom inner border strips.

Step 2 For the side borders, measure the quilt from top to bottom through the middle including the seam allowances, but not the borders just added. Cut the 2-1/2-inch wide **GREEN** side inner border strips to this length. Sew a 2-1/2-inch **BLUE** corner square to both ends of the side border strips; press. Sew the borders to the side edges of the quilt; press.

Step 3 Attach the 3-1/2-inch wide **BLUE/CREAM FLORAL** first middle border strips.

Step 4 Attach the 2-1/2-inch wide **BLUE** second middle border strips.

Step 5 Attach the 5-1/2-inch wide **BLUE/CREAM FLORAL** outer border strips.

Putting It All Together

Cut the 5-1/2 yard length of backing fabric in half crosswise to make 2, 2-3/4 yard lengths. Refer to **Finishing the Quilt** on page 75

Quilting Suggestions:

- Pieced blocks - **TB8 Leaf Quartet**
- **CREAM PRINT** alternate blocks - **TB18 Lady Slipper**
- **BEIGE FLORAL** side triangles - **TB39-12" Triangle Trail**
- **BEIGE FLORAL** corner triangles - **TB39-9" Triangle Trail**
- All borders - quilt as one border with meander design

THIMBLEBERRIES® quilt stencils by Quilting Creations International are available at your local quilt shop.

Binding

Cutting

From **BLUE PRINT**:
- Cut 9, 2-3/4 x 44-inch strips

Sew the binding to the quilt using a 3/8-inch seam allowance. This measurement will produce a 1/2-inch wide finished double binding. Refer to **Binding** and **Diagonal Piecing** on page 75 for complete instructions.

Simply Graphic Twin
75 x 92-inches

General Instructions & Glossary

Yardage is based on 44-inch wide fabric. If your fabric is wider or narrower, it will affect the amount of necessary strips you need to cut in some patterns, and of course, it will affect the amount of fabric you have left over. Generally, Thimbleberries® patterns allow for a little extra fabric so you can confidently cut your pattern pieces with ease.

A rotary cutter, mat, and wide clear acrylic ruler with 1/8-inch markings are needed tools in attaining accuracy. A beginner needs good tools just as an experienced quiltmaker needs good equipment. A 24 x 36-inch cutting mat is a good size to own. It will easily accommodate the average quilt fabrics and will aid in accurate cutting. The acrylic ruler you purchase should be at least 6 x 24-inches and easy to read. Do not purchase a smaller ruler to save money. The large size will be invaluable to your quiltmaking success.

It is often recommended to prewash and press fabrics to test for colorfastness and possible shrinkage. If you choose to prewash, wash in cool water and dry in a cool to moderate dryer. Industry standards actually suggest that line drying is best. Shrinkage is generally very minimal and usually is not a concern. A good way to test your fabric for both shrinkage and colorfastness is to cut a 3-inch square of fabric. Soak the fabric in a white bowl filled with water. Squeeze the water out of the fabric and press it dry on a piece of muslin. If the fabric is going to release color, it will do so either in the water or when it is pressed dry. Remeasure the 3-inch fabric square to see if it has changed size considerably (more than 1/4-inch). If it has, wash, dry, and press the entire yardage. This little test could save you hours in prewashing and pressing.

Read instructions thoroughly before beginning a project. Each step will make more sense to you when you have a general overview of the whole process. Take one step at a time and follow the illustrations. They will often make more sense to you than the words. Take "baby steps" so you don't get overwhelmed by the entire process.

When working with flannel and other loosely woven fabrics, always prewash and dry. These fabrics almost always shrink more.

For piecing, place right sides of the fabric pieces together and use 1/4-inch seam allowances throughout the entire quilt unless otherwise specifically stated in the directions. An accurate seam allowance is the most important part of the quiltmaking process after accurately cutting. All the directions are based on accurate 1/4-inch seam allowances. It is very important to check your sewing machine to see what position your fabric should be to get accurate seams. To test, use a piece of 1/4-inch graph paper, stitch along the quarter-inch line as if the paper were fabric. Make note of where the edge of the paper lines up with your presser foot or where it lines up on the throat plate of your machine. Many quilters place a piece of masking tape on the throat plate to help guide the edge of the fabric. Now test your seam allowance on fabric. Cut 2, 2-1/2-inch squares, place right sides together and stitch along one edge. Press seam allowances in one direction and measure. At this point the unit should measure 2-1/2 x 4-1/2-inches. If it does not, adjust your stitching guidelines and test again. Seam allowances are included in the cutting sizes given in this book.

Pressing is the third most important step in quiltmaking. As a general rule, you should never cross a stitched seam with another seam unless it has been pressed. Therefore, every time you stitch a seam, it needs to be pressed before adding another piece. Often, it will feel like you press as much as you sew, and often that is true. It is very important that you press and not iron the seams. Pressing is a firm, up-and-down motion that will flatten the seams but not distort the piecing. Ironing is a back-and-forth motion and will stretch and distort the small pieces. Most quilters use steam to help the pressing process. The moisture does help and will not distort the shapes as long as the pressing motion is used.

An old-fashioned rule is to press seam allowances in one direction, toward the darker fabric. Often, background fabrics are light in color and pressing toward the darker fabric prevents the seam allowances from showing through to the right side. Pressing seam allowances in one direction is thought to create a stronger seam. Also, for ease in hand quilting, the quilting lines should fall on the side of the seam which is opposite the seam allowance. As you piece quilts, you will find these "rules" to be helpful but not neccesarily always appropriate. Sometimes seams need to be pressed in the opposite direction so the seams of different units will fit together more easily, which quilters refer to as seams "nesting" together. When sewing together two units with opposing seam allowances, use the tip of your seam ripper to gently guide the units under your presser foot. Sometimes it is necessary to re-press the seams to make the units fit together nicely. Always try to achieve the least bulk in one spot and accept that no matter which way you press, it may be a little tricky and it could be a little bulky.

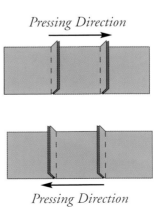

Pressing Direction

Pressing Direction

Squaring Up Blocks

To square up your blocks, first check the seam allowances. This is usually where the problem is, and it is always best to alter within the block rather than trim the outer edges. Next, make sure you have pressed accurately. Sometimes a block can become distorted by ironing instead of pressing.

To trim up block edges, use one of the many clear acrylic squares available on the market. Determine the center of the block; mark with a pin. Lay the square over the block and align as many perpendicular and horizontal lines as you can to the seams in your block. This will indicate where the block is off.

Do not trim all off on one side; this usually results in real distortion of the pieces in the block and the block design. Take a little fabric off all sides until the block is square. When assembling many blocks, it is necessary to make sure all are the same size.

Tools and Equipment

Making beautiful quilts does not require a large number of specialized tools or expensive equipment. My list of favorites is short and sweet and includes the things I use over and over again because they are always accurate and dependable.

I find a long acrylic ruler indispensable for accurate rotary cutting. The ones I like most are an Omnigrid® 6 x 24-inch grid acrylic ruler for cutting long strips and squaring up fabrics and quilt tops and a MasterPiece® 45-degree (8 x 24-inch) ruler for cutting 6- to 8-inch wide borders. I sometimes tape together two 6 x 24-inch acrylic rulers for cutting borders up to 12-inches wide.

A 15-inch Omnigrid® square acrylic ruler is great for squaring up individual blocks and corners of a quilt top, for cutting strips up to 15-inches wide or long, and for trimming side and corner triangles.

I think the markings on my 24 x 36-inch Olfa® rotary cutting mat stay visible longer than on other mats, and the lines are fine and accurate.

The largest size Olfa® rotary cutter cuts through many layers of fabric easily, and isn't cumbersome to use. The 2-1/2-inch blade slices through three layers of backing, batting, and a quilt top like butter.

An 8-inch pair of Gingher shears is great for cutting out appliqué templates and cutting fabric from a bolt or fabric scraps.

I keep a pair of 5-1/2-inch Gingher scissors by my sewing machine so it is handy for both machine work and handwork. This size is versatile and sharp enough to make large and small cuts equally well.

My Grabbit® magnetic pincushion has a surface that is large enough to hold lots of straight pins and a magnet strong enough to keep them securely in place.

Silk pins are long and thin, which means they won't leave large holes in your fabric. I like them because they increase accuracy in pinning pieces or blocks together. It is also easy to press over silk pins.

For pressing individual pieces, blocks, and quilt tops, I use an 18 x 48-inch sheet of plywood covered with several layers of cotton fiberfill and topped with a layer of muslin stapled to the back. The 48-inch length allows me to press an entire width of fabric at one time without the need to reposition it, and the square ends are better than tapered ends on an ironing board for pressing finished quilt tops.

Using Grain

The fabric you purchase still has selvage and before beginning to handle or cut your fabric, it's helpful to be able to recognize and understand its basic characteristics. Fabric is produced in the mill with identifiable grain or direction. These are: lengthwise, crosswise and bias.

The lengthwise grain is the direction that fabric comes off the milling machine, and is parallel to the selvage. This grain of the fabric has the least stretch and the greatest strength.

The crosswise grain is the short distance that spans a bolt's 42-inch to 44-inch width. The crosswise grain, or width of grain, is between two sides called selvages. This grain of the fabric has medium stretch and medium strength.

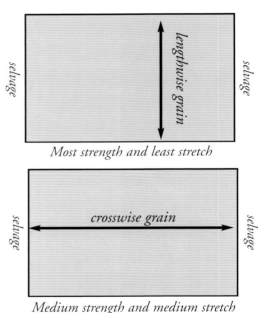

Most strength and least stretch

Medium strength and medium stretch

Avoiding Bias

The 45-degree angle on a piece of fabric is the bias and the direction with the most stretch. I suggest avoiding sewing on the bias until you're confident handling fabric. With practice and careful handling, bias edges can be sewn and are best for making curves.

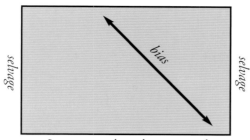

Least strength and most stretch

Rotary Cutting

SAFETY FIRST! The blades of a rotary cutter are very sharp and need to be for accurate cutting. Look at a variety of cutters to find one that feels good in your hand. All quality cutters have a safety mechanism to "close" the cutting blade when not in use. After each cut and before laying the rotary cutter down, close the blade. Soon this will become second nature to you and will prevent dangerous accidents. Always keep cutters out of the sight of children. Rotary cutters are very tempting to fiddle with when they are laying around. When your blade is dull or nicked, change it. Damaged blades do not cut accurately and require extra effort that can also result in slipping and injury. Also, always cut away from yourself for safety.

Squaring Off Fabric

Fold the fabric in half lengthwise matching the selvage edges.

Square off the ends of your fabric before measuring and cutting pieces. This means that the cut edge of the fabric must be exactly perpendicular to the folded edge which creates a 90-degree angle. Align the folded and selvage edges of the fabric with the lines on the cutting board, and place a ruled square on the fold. Place a 6 x 24-inch ruler against the side of the square to get a 90-degree angle. Hold the ruler in place, remove the square, and cut along the edge of the ruler. If you are left-handed, work from the other end of the fabric. Use the lines on your cutting board to help line up fabric, but not to measure and cut strips. Use a ruler for accurate cutting, always checking to make sure your fabric is lined up with horizontal and vertical lines on the ruler.

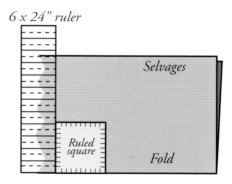

Cutting Strips

When cutting strips or rectangles, cut on the crosswise grain. Strips can then be cut into squares or smaller rectangles.

If your strips are not straight after cutting a few of them, refold the fabric, align the folded and selvage edges with the lines on the cutting board, and "square off" the edge again by trimming to straighten, and begin cutting.

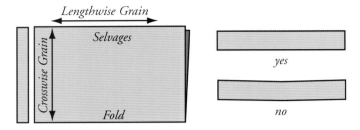

Cutting Bias Strips

When cutting bias strips, trim your yardage on the crosswise grain so the edges are straight. With right sides facing up, fold the yardage on the diagonal. Fold the selvage edge (lengthwise grain) over to meet the cut edge (crosswise grain), forming a triangle. This diagonal fold is the true bias. Position the ruler to the desired strip width from the cut edge and cut one strip. Continue moving the ruler across the fabric cutting parallel strips in the desired widths.

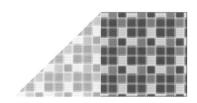

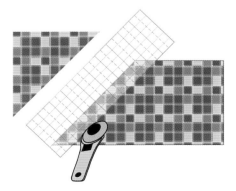

Trimming Side and Corner Triangles

In projects with side and corner triangles, the instructions have you cut side and corner triangles larger than needed. This will allow you to square up the quilt and eliminates the frustration of ending up with pre-cut side and corner triangles that don't match the size of your pieced blocks.

To cut triangles, first cut squares. The project directions will tell you what size to make the squares and whether to cut them in half to make two triangles or to cut them in quarters to make four triangles, as shown in the diagrams. This cutting method will give you side triangles that have the straight grain on the outside edges of the quilt. This is a very important part of quiltmaking that will help stabilize your quilt center.

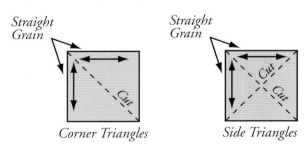

Corner Triangles   Side Triangles

Helpful Hints for Sewing with Flannel

Always prewash and machine dry flannel. This will prevent severe shrinkage after the quilt is made. Some flannels shrink more than others. For this reason, we have allowed approximately 1/4 yard extra for each fabric under the fabric requirements. Treat the more heavily napped side of solid flannels as the right side of the fabric.

Because flannel stretches more than other cotton calicos and because the nap makes them thicker, the quilt design should be simple. Let the fabric and color make the design statement.

Consider combining regular cotton calicos with flannels. The different textures complement each other nicely.

Use a 10 to 12 stitches per inch setting on your machine. A 1/4-inch seam allowance is also recommended for flannel piecing.

When sewing triangle-pieced squares together, take extra care not to stretch the diagonal seam. Trim off the points from the seam allowances to eliminate bulk.

Press gently to prevent stretching pieces out of shape.

Check block measurements as you progress. "Square up" the blocks as needed. Flannel will shift and it is easy to end up with blocks that are misshapen. If you trim and measure as you go, you are more likely to have accurate blocks. If you notice a piece of flannel is stretching more than the others, place it on the bottom when stitching on the

machine. The natural action of the feed dogs will help prevent it from stretching.

Before stitching pieces, strips, or borders together, pin often to prevent fabric from stretching and moving. When stitching longer pieces together, divide the pieces into quarters and pin. Divide into even smaller sections to get more control.

Use a lightweight batting to prevent the quilt from becoming too heavy.

Cutting Triangles from Squares

Cutting accurate triangles can be intimidating for beginners, but a clear acrylic ruler, rotary cutter, and cutting mat are all that are needed to make perfect triangles. The cutting instructions often direct you to cut strips, then squares, and then triangles.

Sewing Layered Strips Together

When you are instructed to layer strips, right sides together, and sew, you need to take some precautions. Gently lay one strip on top of another, carefully lining up the raw edges. Pressing the strips together will hold them together nicely, and a few pins here and there will also help. Be careful not to stretch the strips as you sew them together.

Rod Casing or Sleeve to Hang Quilts

To hang wall quilts, attach a casing that is made of the same fabric as the quilt back. Attach this casing at the top of the quilt, just below the binding. Often, it is helpful to attach a second casing at the bottom of the quilt so you can insert a dowel into it which will help weight the quilt and make it hang free of ripples.

To make a rod casing or "sleeve," cut enough strips of fabric equal to the width of the quilt plus 2-inches for side hems. Generally, 6-inch wide strips will accommodate most rods. If you are using a rod with a larger diameter, increase the width of the strips.

Seam the strips together to get the length needed; press. Fold the strip in half lengthwise, wrong sides together. Stitch the long raw edges together with a 1/4-inch seam allowance. Center the seam on the backside of the sleeve; press. The raw edges of the seam will be concealed when the sleeve is stitched to the back of the quilt. Turn under both of the short raw edges; press and stitch to hem the ends. The final measurement should be about 1/2-inch from the quilt edges.

Pin the sleeve to the back of the quilt so the top edge of the sleeve is just below the binding. Hand stitch the top edge of the sleeve in place, then the bottom edge. Make sure to knot and secure your stitches at each end of the sleeve to make sure it will not pull away from the quilt with use. Slip the rod into the casing. If your wall quilt is not directional, making a sleeve for the bottom edge will allow you to turn your quilt end to end to relieve the stress at the top edge. You could also slip a dowel into the bottom sleeve to help anchor the lower edge of the wall quilt.

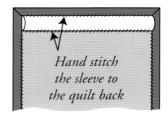

Hand stitch the sleeve to the quilt back

Choosing a Quilting Design

Quilting is such an individual process that it is difficult to recommend designs for each quilt. There are hundreds of quilting stencils available at quilt shops. (Templates are used generally for appliqué shapes; stencils are used for marking quilting designs.) I have developed several Thimbleberries® Quilt Stencils for Quilting Creations that are appropriate for hand quilting and continuous machine quilting.

There are a few suggestions that may help you decide how to quilt your project, depending on how much time you would like to spend quilting. Many quilters now use professional longarm quilting machines or hire someone skilled at running these machines to do the quilting. This, of course, frees up more time to piece quilt tops.

- OUTLINE QUILTING

  follows the outline and accentuates a pieced or appliquéd block by stitching about 1/4-inch away from the seam line or edge of the appliqué shape. It requires no marking. This can be done by hand or machine.

- IN-THE-DITCH QUILTING

  is understated because it nearly disappears in the seam. The stitches are made next to the seam line or along an appliqué edge. It requires no marking and is a good choice for machine quilting or hand quilting.

- BACKGROUND QUILTING

  (crosshatch or grid design) fills large spaces and puts more emphasis on the quilt patterns by making them stand out from the background. Background quilting can be done in straight lines or in a random pattern. This can be done by hand or machine.

- STIPPLE QUILTING (meandering)

  requires no marking to create the random curves that flow across a quilt surface or fill areas of a quilt (that may already have a design) with concentrated quilting stitches. The goal is to avoid having the stitches cross over one another. This is rarely done by hand.

- DESIGN QUILTING

  is often a decorative accent in its own right. Popular designs include feathers, wreaths, cables, and swags which work well in open spaces such as large corner blocks or borders. This can be done by hand or machine.

- ECHO QUILTING

  highlights a motif—usually an appliqué piece. Once the motif is outlined, two or three parallel rows of stitching are added at regular intervals. This can be done by hand or machine.

Quilting Suggestions

Repeat one of the design elements in the quilt as part of the quilting design.

Two or three parallel rows of echo quilting outside an appliqué piece will highlight the shape.

Stipple or meander quilting behind a feather or central motif will make the primary design more prominent.

Look for quilting designs that will cover two or more borders, rather than choosing separate designs for each individual border.

Quilting in-the-ditch of seams is an effective way to get a project quilted without a great deal of time marking the quilt.

Outline Quilting   *In-the-Ditch Quilting*   *Background Quilting*

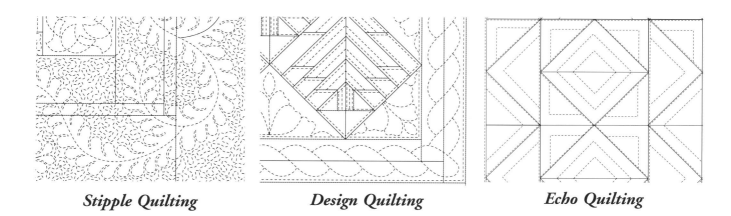

Stipple Quilting   *Design Quilting*   *Echo Quilting*

Marking the Quilting Design

When marking the quilt top, use a marking tool that will be visible on the quilt fabric and yet will be easy enough to remove. Always test your marking tool on a scrap of fabric before marking the entire quilt.

Along with a multitude of commercial marking tools available, you may find that very thin slivers of hand soap (Dial, Ivory, etc.) work well for marking medium to dark color fabrics. The thin lines of soap show up nicely and they are easily removed by simply rubbing gently with a piece of like-colored fabric.

Hints and Helps for Pressing Strip Sets

When sewing strips of fabric together for strip sets, it is important to press the seam allowances nice and flat, usually to the darker fabric. Be careful not to stretch as you press, causing a "rainbow effect." This will affect the accuracy and shape of the pieces cut from the strip set. I like to press on the wrong side first and with the strips perpendicular to the ironing board. Then I flip the piece over and press on the right side to prevent little pleats from forming at the seams. Laying the strip set lengthwise on the ironing board seems to

encourage the rainbow effect, as shown in the diagram.

Avoid this rainbow effect

Borders

NOTE: *Cut borders to the width called for. Always cut border strips a few inches longer than needed, just to be safe. Diagonally piece the border strips together as needed.*

1. With pins, mark the center points along all 4 sides of the quilt. For the top and bottom borders, measure the quilt from left to right through the middle.

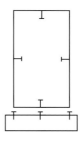

2. Measure and mark the border lengths and center points on the strips cut for the borders before sewing them on.

3. Pin the border strips to the quilt and stitch a 1/4-inch seam. Press the seam allowances toward the border. Trim off excess border lengths.

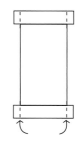

Trim away excess fabric

4. For the side borders, measure your quilt from top to bottom, including the borders just added, to determine the length of the side borders.

5. Measure and mark the side border lengths as you did for the top and bottom borders.

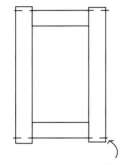

Trim away excess fabric

6. Pin and stitch the side border strips in place. Press and trim the border strips even with the borders just added.

7. If your quilt has multiple borders, measure, mark, and sew additional borders to the quilt in the same manner.

Decorative Stitches

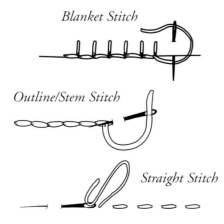

Blanket Stitch

Outline/Stem Stitch

Straight Stitch

Choosing the Backing

The backing of any quilt is just as important to the overall design as the pieced patchwork top. Combine large-scale prints or piece coordinating fabrics together to create an interesting quilt back. Using large pieces of fabric (perhaps three different prints that are the same length as the quilt) or a large piece of fabric that is bordered by compatible prints, keeps the number of seams to a minimum, which speeds up the process. The new 108-inch wide fabric sold on the bolt eliminates the need for seaming entirely. Carefully selected fabrics for a well-constructed backing not only complement a finished quilt, but make it more useful as a reversible accent.

Crib—45 x 60-inches

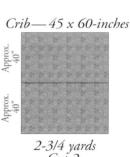

2-3/4 yards
Cut 2,
1-3/8 yard lengths

Twin—72 x 90-inches

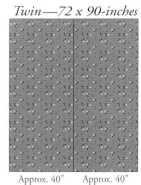

5-1/3 yards
Cut 2, 2-2/3 yard lengths

Double/Full—81 x 96-inches

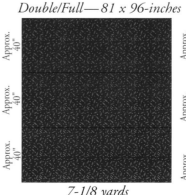

7-1/8 yards
Cut 3, 2-3/8 yard lengths

Queen—90 x 108-inches

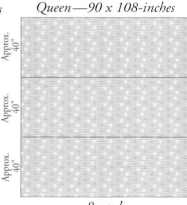

8 yards
Cut 3, 2-2/3 yard lengths

Finishing the Quilt

1. Remove the selvages from the backing fabric. Sew the long edges together and press. Trim the backing and batting so they are 4-inches to 6-inches larger than the quilt top.

2. Mark the quilt top for quilting. Layer the backing, batting, and quilt top. Baste the 3 layers together and quilt.

3. When quilting is complete, remove basting. Hand baste all 3 layers together a scant 1/4-inch from the edge. This hand basting keeps the layers from shifting and prevents puckers from forming when adding the binding. Trim excess batting and backing fabric even with the edge of the quilt top. Add the binding as shown below.

Binding and Diagonal Piecing

1. Diagonally piece the binding strips. Fold the strip in half lengthwise, wrong sides together, and press.

Diagonal Piecing

Stitch diagonally

Trim to 1/4-inch seam allowance

Press seam open

2. Unfold and trim one end at a 45-degree angle. Turn under the edge 3/8-inch and press. Refold the strip.

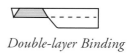

Double-layer Binding

3. With raw edges of the binding and quilt top even, stitch with a 3/8-inch seam allowance, starting 2-inches from the angled end.

4. Miter the binding at the corners. As you approach a corner of the quilt, stop sewing 3/8-inch from the corner of the quilt.

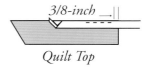

Quilt Top

5. Clip the threads and remove the quilt from under the presser foot. Flip the binding strip up and away from the quilt, then fold the binding down even with the raw edge of the quilt. Begin sewing at the upper edge. Miter all 4 corners in this manner.

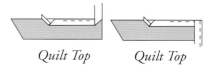

Quilt Top   *Quilt Top*

6. Trim the end of the binding so it can be tucked inside of the beginning binding about 1/2-inch. Finish stitching the seam.

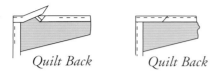

Quilt Back   *Quilt Back*

7. Turn the folded edge of the binding over the raw edges and to the back of the quilt so that the stitching line does not show. Hand sew the binding in place, folding in the mitered corners as you stitch.

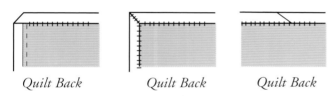

Quilt Back   *Quilt Back*   *Quilt Back*

Glossary

Appliqué The sewing technique for attaching pieces (appliqués) of fabric onto a background fabric. Appliqués may be stitched to the background by hand, using a blind stitch, or by machine, using a satin stitch or a blind hemstitch.

Backing The bottom layer of a quilt consisting of one whole piece of fabric or several fabrics joined together.

Basting The technique for joining layers of fabric or the layers of a quilt with safety pins (pin basting) or large stitches (hand basting). The pinning or stitching is temporary and is removed after permanent stitching.

Batting A layer of filler placed between two pieces of fabric to form a quilt. Its thickness and fiber content varies.

Bias The grain of woven fabric that is at a 45-degree angle to the selvages. The bias grain has more stretch and is less stable than the crosswise or lengthwise grain.

Bias strips Strips of fabric cut on the bias and joined to make one continuous strip for binding that can easily be positioned around curved edges.

Binding The strip of fabric used to cover the outside edges—top, batting and backing—of a quilt.

Block A basic unit, usually square and often repeated, of a quilt top.

Borders The framing on a quilt that serves to visually hold in the design and give the eye a stopping point.

Crosscutting Cutting fabric strips into smaller units, such as squares or rectangles.

Crosswise grain The threads running perpendicular to the selvage across the width of a woven fabric.

Cutting mat Surface used for rotary cutting that protects the tabletop and keeps the fabric from shifting while cutting. Often mats are labeled as self-healing, meaning the blade does not leave slash marks or grooves in the surface even after repeated use.

Double-fold binding Binding made from a fabric strip that is folded in half before being attached to the quilt. Also, referred to as French-fold binding.

Finished size The measurement of a completed block or quilt.

Free-motion or machine quilting
A process of quilting done with the feed dogs disengaged and using a darning presser foot so the quilt can be moved freely on the machine bed in any direction.

Grain The direction of woven fabric. The crosswise grain is from selvage to selvage. The lengthwise grain runs parallel to the selvage and is stronger. The bias grain is at a 45-degree angle and has the greatest amount of stretch.

Hand quilting Series of running stitches made through all layers of a quilt with needle and thread.

Hanging sleeve Tube of fabric that is attached to the quilt back. A wooden dowel is inserted through the fabric tube to hang the quilt. It is also called a rod pocket and used with a board or rod as a support to hang a quilt on the wall.

Inner border A strip of fabric, usually more narrow than the outer border, that frames the quilt center.

Layering Placing the quilt top, batting and quilt backing on top of each other in layers.

Lengthwise grain The threads running parallel to the selvage in a woven fabric.

Longarm quilting A quilting machine used by professional quilters in which the quilt is held taut on a frame that allows the quilter to work on a large portion of the quilt at a time. The machine head moves freely, allowing the operator to use free-motion to quilt in all directions.

Machine quilting Series of stitches made through all layers of a quilt sandwich with a sewing machine.

Marking tools A variety of pens, pencils and chalks that can be used to mark fabric pieces or a quilt top.

Mitered seam A 45-degree angle seam.

Outer border A strip of fabric that is joined to the edges of the quilt top to finish or frame it.

Pieced border Blocks or pieced units sewn together to make a single border unit that is then sewn to the quilt center.

Piecing The process of sewing pieces of fabric together.

Pressing Using an iron with an up and down motion to set stitches and flatten a seam allowance, rather than sliding it across the fabric.

Quilt center The quilt top before borders are added.

Quilt top Top layer of a quilt usually consisting of pieced blocks.

Quilting The small running stitches made through the layers of a quilt (quilt top, batting and backing) to form decorative patterns on the surface of the quilt and hold the layers together.

Quilting stencils Quilting patterns with open areas through which a design is transferred onto a quilt top. May be purchased or made from sturdy, reusable template plastic.

Rotary cutter Tool with a sharp, round blade attached to a handle that is used to cut fabric. The blade is available in different diameters.

Rotary cutting The process of cutting fabric into strips and pieces using a revolving blade rotary cutter, a thick, clear acrylic ruler and a special cutting mat.

Running stitches A series of in-and-out stitches used in hand quilting.

Seam allowance The 1/4-inch margin of fabric between the stitched seam and the raw edge.

Selvage The lengthwise finished edge on each side of the fabric.

Slipstitch A hand stitch used for finishing such as sewing binding to a quilt where the thread is hidden by slipping the needle between a fold of fabric and tacking down with small stitches.

Squaring up or straightening fabric The process of trimming the raw edge of the fabric so it creates a 90-degree angle with the folded edge of the fabric. Squaring up is also a term used when trimming a quilt block.

Strip sets Two or more strips of fabric, cut and sewn together along the length of the strips.

Triangle-pieced square The square unit created when two 90-degree triangles are sewn together on the diagonal.

Unfinished size The measurement of a block before the 1/4-inch seam allowance is sewn or the quilt is quilted and bound.

Thimbleberries® Books by Lynette Jensen

Thimbleberries® books are available at book stores, fabric and craft stores. If you are unable to find them at your favorite retailer, contact Landauer Corporation at 1-800-557-2144 or visit www.landauercorp.com

**Thimbleberries® Quilts
for My Sister's House**
ISBN: 978-1-890621-57-5

**Thimbleberries®
Learning to Quilt**
ISBN: 978-1-890621-51-3

**Thimbleberries® Quilting
a Patchwork Garden**
ISBN: 978-1-890621-62-9

**Thimbleberries®
You're Invited**
ISBN: 978-0-9800688-1-8

**Thimbleberries® New
Collection of Classic Quilts**
ISBN: 978-1-890621-98-8

**Thimbleberries®
Collection of Classic Quilts**
ISBN: 978-1-890621-88-9

**Thimbleberries® Four Seasons
of Calendar Table Toppers**
ISBN: 978-0-9770166-8-6

**Thimbleberries®
Quilting for Harvest**
ISBN: 978-1-890621-16-2

**Thimbleberries® Big
Book of Quilt Blocks**
ISBN: 978-1-932533-05-7

**Thimbleberries®
Beginner's Luck**
ISBN: 978-0-972558-01-3

**Thimbleberries®
Pint-Size Traditions**
ISBN: 978-1-932533-03-3

**Thimbleberries® Oh Sew
Cozy Flannel Quilts**
ISBN: 978-1-932533-04-0